YOUR
JOURNEY
INTO
ETERNITY

LIFE FOR THE NEXT 1,000 YEARS

PERRY STONE

YOUR JOURNEY INTO ETERNITY: LIFE FOR THE NEXT 1,000 YEARS

Published by Voice of Evangelism Ministries
P. O. Box 3595
Cleveland TN 37320
423.478.3456
www.perrystone.org

Unmarked Scripture quotations are from the King James Version of the Bible.

Scripture quotations marked NKJV are from the New Kings James Version of the Bible. Copyright © 1979, 1980, 1982 by Thomas Nelson, Inc., publishers. Used by permission.

First Edition © 2023

Printed in the United States of America

ISBN: 978-0-9895618-2-2

Cover Design & Layout: Michael Dutton

The illustration of the Millennial Temple featured on the cover is used by permission from International School of the Word. To access in-depth teachings on the Millennial Temple and other courses visit ISOW.org.

CONTENTS

INTRODUCTION

I stood beside the bedside of my precious grandfather, John Bava, a former coal miner, singer, music publisher, and pastor of a church that he personally built and pastored for decades. He had just turned eighty-four years of age. He was about to take the ultimate trip from earth's pain to the bliss of a heavenly paradise, joining the souls of his family members who had made their own journey years before. Soon his spirit would leave his body, and in seconds he would make an entrance into glory.

I had been ministering in Zambia, Africa when I received a call from my wife telling me that Granddad was not doing well after surgery. Tests indicated he had experienced several strokes. His eyes were closed and he could not speak, yet his vital signs revealed that he was still with us.

I cut short the ministry in Africa and took a flight back to the United States. When I arrived at the hospital, I stood over his bed where the only sounds in the room were coming from electronic medical devices. After spending two days with him, I softly spoke into his ear, "Granddad, I have to go back home. I'm praying for you, and I'll see you again." With his eyelids closed, a single tear formed on the inside of his left eye. I knew he had heard me.

His doctor told us to talk to him, as hearing is the last sense to go before a person passes. Granddad had heard us at his bedside singing songs that he wrote. He heard us talking about what it would be like arriving in the presence of God. His heart rate increased on the monitor when someone told one of his jokes. It was as though he was laughing along with us.

Somehow, he also knew it would be my last earthly visit with him, until I joined him and the family when my time on earth is finished.

With much sadness, my wife and I returned to Cleveland, Tennessee. My sister was in the room when Granddad's heart rate flatlined on the monitor. She said that an overwhelming peace came into the room. In a few minutes, his earthly shell lay silent on the bed. Before his body was rolled out of the room, his soul and spirit had arrived at the place he had sung and preached about for over sixty years.

When word arrived to me, I immediately thought of one of his noted songs about heaven, recorded by country music artist Ricky Van Shelton:

> Heaven is a city, built by jewels rare
>
> Its beauty is a splendor to behold
>
> But if you neglect salvation, you'll never enter in
>
> You'll never, ever walk on streets of gold.

He made the journey. Your journey and mine will come one day. Unless we're alive to experience the return of Christ, we will become part of the great cloud of witnesses (Heb. 12:1), those referred to by Paul as "the dead in Christ" (1 Thess. 4:16). Our spirits will remain in paradise; then one day, Christ will make a sudden appearance in the air, at an event that theologians term "the rapture." The dead in Christ will rise from the grave and receive a new body that will never perish, and their spirits will be joined with their new bodies. Those believers who are alive will be instantly changed from mortality to immortality.

From that moment on, we will join other believers throughout the ages who have accepted the gift of eternal life. We will experience the time of our lives, as our lives will just begin. We will be full of joy, and every adventure will be mindboggling.

So many events that happen after the return of Christ are seldom taught and often misunderstood. Those are the topics included in this book—the mysterious truths to be explained, especially to a generation with many questions.

For some, death is a mystery. From a biblical standpoint, death is not just the cessation of human life; it is the separation of the eternal from the earthly. Death includes the separation of the soul and spirit from the earthly body. The body will be placed in its grave to decay, but the soul and spirit immediately transition from one location to the next.

In the next life are two completely opposite destinations. In Scripture, one is located *up* from the earth (heaven and its paradise), and the other is described as *below* or *down,* thus being positioned somewhere beneath the surface of the earth. The Hebrew and Greek words found in the Bible for this underworld of departed souls are sheol, hades, gehenna, and tartarus. Several of these words translate in the King James Version of the Bible as *hell.*

This book focuses on the upper celestial realm. It reveals what occurs at the time of death for believers who will be transported to the heavenly resting place called paradise. It includes insight into our return to Jerusalem to rule with Christ for a thousand years, the heavenly judgments, and the new heaven and new earth. Many questions will be answered, and I believe you will gain valuable wisdom, knowledge, and understanding of future events for believers.

Grandad Bava loved to play an accordion and sing that old Gospel song, "When We All Get to Heaven." He concluded many services at his church in Maryland singing, "When the battle's over, we shall wear a crown." We all have an inescapable appointment with death (Heb. 9:27). If you are prepared, it will be an exciting time. If you are not prepared, death is a frightening experience. It is my hope that this book will help you with that preparation.

CHAPTER 1

THE SPLIT-SECOND YOUR INNER EYES ARE OPENED

In 2011, three weeks after my father's seventy-eighth birthday, he found himself spending the final week of his life in a nursing care center in our town. I spent nights at his bedside, praying and holding his hand. Eventually, he closed his eyes and became mostly unresponsive. Soon he would make the great exodus from this world to the next.

The family was together in the room one night when Dad suddenly opened his eyes and looked around as though searching for someone. It seemed he received a sudden surge of energy and life. Then he shut his eyes and never opened them again. I thought to myself, "What just happened? He seemed to be fully alert."

I believe his spirit was being alerted to the angels coming. I snapped a picture on my phone of Dad lying on the bed, now seemingly unaware of us. The picture showed a bright beam of light on his right, coming from the wall close to his head. I sent the photo to Pastor Tommy Bates. He replied, "That's the angel coming to get him!" I believe it.

The Christian church's testimony file is filled with wonderful stories of men, women, and children who, moments before death, pierced the veil into the invisible world. This included the ability to see angels.

Some Christians who still maintained mental alertness to the end have described angelic looking men dressed in white, some with wings and others without, who entered the room and, at times, stood near their bed. I believe these are angels commissioned from the third heaven, by God Almighty Himself, to release the souls and spirits from the bodies of those who are dying and carry them into the eternal kingdom of heaven.

This is evident in Luke 16. When the beggar at the rich man's gate died, angels carried him into Abraham's bosom (Luke 16:22). In this reference, the word *angels* is plural, which means that more than one angel assisted in the transition.

What occurs near death that enables a dying believer to hear music, see loved ones who have passed, or see angels arriving to supernaturally escort a believer to the next life?

SENSES ON FULL ALERT

The living human body has five senses—hearing, seeing, smelling, tasting, and touching. Did you know that the soul and spirit of each person also has those same five senses? In John's vision of heaven, those who were there could see, hear, sing, speak, reason, and worship. They were fully aware and alert. In Luke 16, the rich man could feel heat and pain. The beggar could feel peace and comfort. Conversations occurred.

Jesus said, "He that has ears to hear, let him hear" (Matt. 11:15). We all have ears to hear—natural ears on each side of our head, and spiritual ears connected to our spirit.

Paul spoke of the eyes of your understanding being enlightened (Eph.1:18). This verse refers, not to the natural eyes, but to the eyes of the human spirit that are veiled or closed and must be enlightened (illuminated) to bring understanding.

SEEING THE INVISIBLE AT DEATH

Something supernatural occurs moments before a person passes from the earthly realm to the heavenly realm. The veil is removed from their natural eyes and their spiritual ears are opened. If the person is still alert, a believer might tell those in the room that they hear beautiful music or people singing. In every case I have known, the only person in the room who can hear the inaudible sounds is the one who will soon depart this earth for their heavenly home, from where those sounds are originating.

The same holds true when the dying person sees someone standing near them or their bed. The dying believer might ask a question such as, "Who is that nice man with you?" On several occasions, my father spoke about the pre-death experiences of his relatives who were followers of Christ. During their final moments of life, they would see a person they did not know, or two men they had never met, standing in the room. Dad believed they were seeing angels that had arrived to take their soul and spirit to the heavenly paradise.

Human eyes and ears are set on earthly sights and sounds. While living in a mortal body, people operate in the realm of the flesh. The desires of our flesh are carnal—that is, worldly or of the flesh, according to Scripture. The spirit of a person is willing to obey God, but the flesh is weak (Matt. 26:41).

When people are not redeemed and in covenant with Christ, their flesh will control their lives, and their spirits will remain dead to the voice of God and insensitive to spiritual truths. However, when the spirit is preparing to make its final exit from the human shell in which it dwells, the senses become alert to the unseen realm. This also happens to those who see that they are headed to the underworld. Hardhearted sinners have described darkness, dark tunnels, a feeling of heat or fire, or frightening and unearthly creatures standing nearby.

REMOVING THE EYE SCALES

When God created Adam in the Garden of Eden, He breathed into him the breath of life. Adam and God literally talked to one other, and Adam heard God's voice in the cool of the day. We know there are times that the Lord appeared to humans in the form of a man. Theologically this is called a theophany.

Such an appearance occurred when the Lord and two angels came to Abraham's tent and ate with him (Gen. 18). Later, both angelic messengers journeyed to Sodom to connect with Lot. They were given power to blind the men of Sodom, so that the men could not grasp the doorknob to enter Lot's house (Gen. 19:11). These angels looked so much like normal men that the men of Sodom assumed they were two traveling strangers who stopped in the city to spend the night. This was one of those rare occasions when angels took on human form and all humans in the city could see them.

When God met with Adam and walked among the trees in the garden, did God manifest in a human-type form, or were Adam's eyes completely open to both the natural and spirit world? When Adam and Eve were expelled from the garden, God placed angelic beings called cherubim and a flaming sword to guard the east entrance to the garden. This prevented the fallen couple from reentering the garden and eating from the tree of life, thereby living forever in a sinful condition (Gen. 3:22-24).

The implication in Scripture is that Adam could see God and the cherubim—all spirits that are invisible to the veiled human eyes. When Adam sinned, his eyes were opened to see that he and Eve were naked. *His eyes were opened; but at the same time, they became veiled.* Before they sinned, Adam and Eve could see both the visible and invisible realms, which is why they could see God and angels. After they sinned, the invisible world became hidden from sight, and the things they did not want to see or experience (such as death) were made manifest.

Twice in the Bible, some type of scales had to be removed from the eyes before the person could see into the invisible realm. When the Syrian army descended on the hill of Dothan to take Elisha captive, the old prophet saw a heavenly army that neither the enemy nor his loyal servant could see. Only after Elisha prayed for his servant were his eyes opened, and he saw that they both were surrounded by an army of angels riding in chariots of fire (2 Kings 6:17).

Elisha himself had his own spiritual eyes opened when his mentor, the prophet Elijah, was transported to heaven. Elijah instructed Elisha, "If you *see* me when I am taken up... you will receive a double portion."

Not far from them, in Jericho, fifty sons of the prophets saw Elijah go up "in a whirlwind" (2 Kings 2). However, Elisha saw more than the whirlwind; he also saw horses and chariots of fire, as Elijah enjoyed a supernatural escort from earth to heaven (2 Kings 2). The fifty sons saw the *natural* realm—the whirlwind. Elisha's eyes were opened to see the *invisible* world.

This requires more than a good set of eyes and 20/20 vision. Something about our natural vision keeps us from continually seeing supernatural beings. Eyes see the natural realm, while the spirit can perceive the supernatural realm. As death approaches, before the spirit leaves the body, often the person's spirit can pierce the veil and *see* what is in the room.

NO PAIN IN THE PROCESS

The person experiencing the death transition might have spent weeks, months, or even years in severe pain and suffering. Certain diseases cause a level of physical pain that can be unbearable. Paul made it clear, however, that the bodily transition to heaven is not a painful experience. The death and resurrection of Christ provided a smooth transition from the earthly to the heavenly realm for every person whose name is inscribed in the Lamb's Book of Life.

Speaking of death, Paul wrote, "Oh death, where is thy sting? O grave, where is thy victory?" (1 Cor. 15:55). The Greek word for sting is *kentron*, which refers to something being pricked that causes a sudden pain. There is no sting or pain for a follower of Christ, once the spirit is lifted out of the body and escorted away by angels. Death is the ultimate healing. Once we arrive in the heavenly paradise, from that moment and forever, there will be no more sickness, no more death, no more pain, and no more sorrow (Rev. 21:4). For a true follower of Christ, the transition from earth to heaven is the ultimate escape.

The characteristics of a person's spirit are similar to those of the physical body. This is how, according to 1 Corinthians 13:12, we will know and be known (in heaven) as we were known (on earth). At death, the spirit is separated from the body in a manner similar to a hand being pulled from a glove. The glove is not the hand, and the hand is not the glove. However, the hand fits in the glove, and the glove has the form of the hand.

Your spirit looks like you. Your spirit has the same hands, arms, legs, torso, facial features, and so on. The spirit brings life to the body. Think of the air that fills an empty balloon. Let the air out and the form collapses. Similarly, without the spirit, the body will become lifeless and eventually return to the dust.

RECOGNIZING CHRIST IN HEAVEN

When Christ was raised from the dead, some who knew Him before His crucifixion and had even traveled with Him did not recognize Him after the resurrection. That seems strange, especially with Mary. She took spices to anoint His body, and upon arriving she saw angels in the tomb announcing that Christ is alive.

Moments later, when she saw Christ, she mistook Him for a gardener, as this tomb was in a garden and was owned by a rich disciple of Christ (John 19:41). Only after He called her name did she recognize this apparent stranger. Some scholars suggest that the crucifixion changed certain aspects of Christ's physical appearance, including the possibility of His hair becoming white (which it presently is, according to Revelation 1:14).

Two of Christ's disciples—one is believed to have been Luke—were walking together on a Roman road from Jerusalem to the village of Emmaus, a distance of approximately seven miles. Christ met them and began a discussion from the Torah and prophets, explaining the many predictions that revealed the Messiah. During the entire walk and conversation, neither disciple perceived that the stranger was Christ. Suddenly we read, "And their eyes were opened, and they knew him; and he vanished out of their sight" (Luke 24:31).

It is odd that neither Mary nor these two men, who had personally seen and heard Christ minister for many months or years, would at first not recognize Him.

There were others, including the Apostle John, who saw Christ in a vision about sixty-four years after Christ's ascension. John immediately knew that the person he was seeing, with hair white as snow, eyes like a flame of fire, feet like fine brass, and a countenance like the sun, was not an angel, but indeed was Jesus Christ (Rev. 1).

In all the time that John knew and followed Christ, had he ever seen Him with brass feet or eyes like fire? No, and if Christ had physically appeared in this form, I doubt many children would have wanted to come near Him, or have Him lay a hand on them. When John saw Him in this glorious form, he fell at His feet as one being dead (Rev. 1:17).

In Acts 7, Stephen was the first martyr that Scripture identifies in the church in Jerusalem. Before he was pelted with rocks and killed, one of his final statements was, "Behold, I see the heavens opened, and the Son of man standing on the right hand of God" (Acts 7:56). We can assume that Stephen had previously, at some point, met Christ in person. Here he sees Christ standing on God's right side, where He is presently positioned as the High Priest in heaven. Christ's appearance should have been similar to John's visions in Revelation chapter 1. Yet, Stephen saw the heavens open and immediately recognized Christ.

Prior to the crucifixion, Christ had a recognizable physical appearance that was familiar to everyone close to Him. If He walked into a room, they knew that Jesus showed up. His death and three days in the tomb should not have changed His appearance so much that He was not recognizable, except for the scars in His feet, hands, and side, which distinguished Him from all others. After His resurrection, there must have been some changes that, at times, made it difficult for His closest friends and associates to recognize Him.

A second point is that the sound and tone of His voice did not change. When He spoke, Mary knew it was Christ.

If there was any doubt that Christ was standing in their midst, unbelief melted like fog in sunlight when He revealed the scars from His crucifixion. The scars that remained, even on His resurrected body, were the proof that Thomas needed to cry out, "My Lord and my God" (John 20:28).

THE OLD WILL BECOME YOUNG AGAIN

If you are over sixty, how many times have you said to yourself, "If only I could go back to the age of thirty!" From the testimony of hundreds of people who had near-death experiences and saw deceased family members and friends, there is strong evidence that believers turn back the clock when we die. Once we breathe our last breath and our spirit leaves our body, we will appear in the heavenly paradise as a much younger person than we were the moment we died. The only exception I am aware of is children who died. By the time people have lived into their 80s and 90s, they are showing their age and moving a lot slower. I know of nobody, and I do mean nobody, who is looking to arrive in heaven that age.

Since the human spirit is a replica of the person's body, the spirit will be recognized by those who knew the person on earth. I believe that once a person reaches their individual level of physical maturity, the spirit, which has grown inside the body as the body has grown, ceases to age at a certain point. Only the body of mortal flesh continues to age. This might explain why older people often express that they feel younger than their bodies reflect.

Based on hundreds of firsthand accounts where family members had an experience—a dream, vision, or near-death event—that allowed them to see a loved one in heaven who died at an advanced age, they report that none looked old. Most say they looked as they did when they were in their early 30s.

This is interesting, because in the days of the Jewish tabernacle and temples, no man could enter the priesthood until he was thirty years old (Num. 4:3-39). Christ did not engage in public ministry until He was about thirty years of age (Luke 3:23). When God formed Adam, he was created as a full-grown man. Jewish tradition suggests that Adam would have appeared to be about thirty years old. The body ages. However, the spirit within a living person is eternal, and therefore is not impacted by advanced age.

Two facts are evident. The mortal physical body of a person grows older and eventually shows wrinkles, aches and pains, sickness, and other signs of aging, all of which are part of the human life cycle. But the unusual molecular structure of a human spirit does not show signs of aging. This should be good news for all of us, knowing we can leave the aging behind when we get to heaven.

FOR ETERNITY, SPIRITS NEVER AGE

God is a Spirit (John 4:24). He is called "the Ancient of Days" three times by the prophet Daniel (Dan. 7:9, 13, 22). It is humorous that the Aramaic word used in Daniel to describe God as ancient is *attiq* and can be translated as "antique," which is something of great age with great value. God, because He is Spirit, has never changed in power, ability, or appearance.

Angels are spirits. This includes Michael and Gabriel, whose past earthly assignments included battling over Moses' body (Jude 9), assisting Daniel in Babylon (Daniel 10), and announcing the births of John the Baptist and Christ (Luke 1-2). In the future great tribulation, Michael will cast Satan from the second heaven to the earth (Rev. 12:7-10).

Moses lived 3,500 years ago and Daniel 2,600 years ago. Christ was born to Mary about 2,000 years ago. The tribulation will arrive in the future. Michael and Gabriel were angels prior to Adam's creation, and they still are active today and will continue to be active in the future. Since angels are spirits, Michael and Gabriel have not aged or become weak and feeble.

CHOOSING YOUR AGE IN HEAVEN

One unusual story may explain why people appear to be a certain age in heaven. While ministering at a church in Indiana years ago, a gentleman told me an amazing story. He shared that his wife had passed away with cancer and how it impacted him and his children, especially his oldest daughter, who was grieving terribly.

Then an unusual experience occurred. One night the daughter saw her mother appear in her bedroom. The mother told her daughter not to grieve anymore because she is in heaven, and it is far beyond anything words can express.

The daughter suddenly was overcome with peace. She noticed that her mother looked healthy, strong, and young–nothing like she had appeared when she was sick. The daughter was thinking how beautiful her mother looked, when the mother expressed that upon arriving in heaven, she had been asked by an angel how old she wanted to look. She wanted to look as she did when she was thirty-one years of age.

Following this brief encounter, the daughter was excited to share this experience with her father. He was so moved with joy that he told his wife's best friend, who had been with her during her suffering and until the time of her death. The friend was shocked, as she had never shared the following story with the family until she heard of this encounter.

The friend told the father that there was a picture of his wife in the room where she had been lying in bed when she was very sick. The picture was taken when his wife was thirty-one years of age. She had expressed to her friend, "When I get to heaven, I hope I look like I did in that picture."

Neither the daughter nor the husband had been aware of this story, but it confirmed the authenticity of the vision the daughter had seen of her mother.

NEAR-DEATH EXPERIENCES

Many Christians around the world have come back to life after a near-death experience where the spirit left the body and was permitted to see into or enter the heavenly realm. When a person has a true near-death encounter, the skeptics run to the front of the line to try to discredit the testimony.

For years, medical professionals, scientists, and curiosity seekers have studied such experiences, hoping to offer some explanation for this phenomenon. Some of these professionals possess a root of faith, but many of the people researching this are atheists or agnostics, so their feeble theories always omit the supernatural God factor. Some are skeptical about a belief in life beyond the grave, or the existence of a human soul and spirit that mirrors a person's body. Despite the skeptics, it is reasonable to state that there are far too many people with personal near-death experiences to simply claim that such events are a mirage caused by the release of a brain chemical, as some professionals theorize.

Near-death experiences have occurred during events such as a car accident, a shooting, surgery, and cardiac arrest. In such cases, the body experiences trauma that causes the heart to stop and the person to die for a length of time—minutes or longer. They know that their spirit has left their body, because they can observe themselves in the traumatic situation and perhaps even watch someone try to revive them. As they hover above the situation, they can see the sights, hear the sounds, and observe events happening below them, all the while thinking that they must have died.

I have spoken with many people who informed their physician that they left their body and went to a place of bliss and beauty. Others fearfully related that they entered a place of darkness, gloom, and even fire. Some physicians claim that this is a result of religious upbringing that emphasized heaven or taught a fear of hell. Others claim it's a result of chemical release.

If the experience had been caused by a flood of chemicals to the brain, then it seems that practically everyone having a near death experience would find themselves in the same situation. If everyone carried the same religious beliefs, and if everybody having a near-death experience saw the very same things, then perhaps the chemical release theory would have some validity. But that does not happen.

Some who never believed in God have seen a divine being engulfed in light; at times, the closer they drew to the being, the more it changed into a demonic creature. Second Corinthians 11:14 reveals that Satan disguises himself as an angel of light, so it's important to align your experience with the Word of God.

Others who spent their lifetime mocking the existence of hell suddenly found themselves in a place that eerily mirrored the biblical description of hell. If the medical theories were true, it would mean that Christians would experience hell in the same manner as a non-believer. But most Christians see only heaven since that is their promised destination.

Witnesses testify of seeing both heaven and hell when their spirit leaves their body during a near-death experience. Some of these encounters are mentioned throughout this book.

Far too many people have testimonies and documented experiences proving that another world exists outside of our visible world. The Bible is the ultimate, inspired source that details the dual worlds that exists beyond the grave, thus confirming what so many of these people have experienced.

CHAPTER 2

THE FINALITY OF A SPIRIT RETURNING TO GOD

Humans are three-part beings, regardless of age or size, and whether still in the womb or lying on a deathbed. Each has a physical body that will grow older every day; a soul that operates the senses and emotions; and an eternal spirit that fills the space within the body, the way air fills a balloon. Remove the air from a balloon and you have a lifeless shell of a balloon. Remove the spirit from the body and you are left with a lifeless body.

Paul revealed the three parts when he wrote, "Now may the God of peace Himself sanctify you completely; and may your whole spirit, soul, and body be preserved blameless at the coming of our Lord Jesus Christ" (1 Thess. 5:23).

Solomon provided interesting insight into death. He spoke of a mysterious silver cord: "Remember your Creator before the silver cord is loosed." Then he wrote, "The dust will return to the earth as it was, and the spirit will return to God who gave it" (Eccl. 12:6-7).

In the womb, an umbilical cord connects the infant to the mother and supplies oxygen and nutrients to the growing baby. When cut, the mother no longer supplies oxygen or nutrients, and the baby then breathes and eats without the benefit of that connecting cord.

Similarly, there is an invisible silver cord that connects the human spirit to its body. When the cord is severed, the spirit is separated from the body, and the body without the spirit is dead (James 2:26).

Death is more than the heart no longer beating. Death occurs when an angel of God cuts your spirit loose from the restraints of your physical body that has operated with limitations on the earth. The body becomes weak, sick, and tired. Eventually it dies. But the human spirit has no limitations. Paul noted, "Though the outward man (the body) perishes, the inner man (the spirit) is renewed day by day" (2 Cor. 4:16).

WATCHING THE MONITORS

In April 1997, my grandfather, John Bava, was taken to the hospital where he underwent surgery. During that time, the surgeon discovered that he had a severe heart problem. He also suffered three strokes and was never able to recover.

I had been preaching out of the country and arrived several days later to his hospital room. I knew that he was alive and his spirit aware because of the reaction on the monitors. When we spoke to him, sang to him, or told one of his jokes, his heart rate increased significantly. He could hear us, but he couldn't verbally respond. His doctor told us that, even when a person is dying, hearing is the last sense to go.

We had a different experience with my mother. After twelve days in the hospital, the nurses said she was showing improvement in the intensive care unit, and they were attempting to wean her from the ventilator. However, while we were sitting in church on a Tuesday night, a message came to my wife's phone from a nurse, suggesting that we immediately come to the hospital. Mom had a heart attack and died. Medical personnel spent ten minutes shocking her back to life, but they did not expect her to live long.

By the time we arrived, they had heavily sedated her, and the medical equipment was keeping her alive. She was unresponsive. As we talked to her, I observed the monitors. The lines remained the same without any change when we spoke. Before long, her blood pressure monitor dropped to zero, and other vitals were dropping as well. I think her spirit left earlier and she got a glimpse of the other side and didn't want to come back.

At some point that night, our mother reunited with her husband, her parents, and a host of other saints of God she had met during her lifetime who made the journey ahead of her.

WE ALL ARE A LIVING SOUL

Adam was created a full-grown man, having never entered the world through the womb of a woman. Adam's body was formed from the dust of the ground, but it remained a lifeless lump of clay until God breathed into his nostrils the breath of life (Gen 2:7). The breath of God brought Adam to life and made him a living soul.

The name Adam in Hebrew means *a ruddy or reddish color,* likely because Adam was created from red dirt or clay. However, he was a life-less lump until God breathed *out* and Adam breathed *in*. James wrote, "For as the body without the spirit is dead, so faith without works is dead also" (James 2:26). This verse holds a powerful revelation about death.

Death does not happen just because the heart stops beating or the breathing stops. This is part of the death process, but this is not death itself. As long as the spirit remains in the body, the body is still alive.

Stories abound of people who were involved in accidents that resulted in a coma or their inability to speak, open their eyes, or move for weeks or months. Often the doctors had given up hope for recovery. Yet, they were still alive on the inside because their spirit remained confined in their body.

One of my friends was Evangelist Richard Madison, who was in a horrific car accident years ago. He was ready to be sent to the morgue when a trauma physician at Vanderbilt heard a voice telling him to try again. Richard survived and spent twenty-seven days in a coma. During that time, doctors still advised the family to plan his funeral.

Through God's mercy and after much prayer, he awoke from the coma and was raised up from his death bed. God told him to preach, and Richard ministered for many years.

Richard talked about some unusual things that happened while he was in a coma. On several occasions his spirit left his body, walked the halls of the hospital, and saw things that were happening. One time his spirit walked into the hospital chapel and saw his mother in a blue dress, pleading with God to heal him. Other times he could hear conversations of doctors, nurses, and visitors standing near his bed. He recalled a nurse cursing him because she had to work New Year's Eve and missed a big party. When he came out of the coma, he told the nurse what she said.

To a casual observer, Richard appeared to be a dying, lifeless man who was being kept alive by medical devices. The coma impacted his body and mind, but it had no impact on his spirit. It is impossible to destroy the human spirit. The spirit is eternal, and that is why both eternal life and eternal punishment are without end.

WHAT HAPPENS AT A RESURRECTION?

Scripture records several individuals who, through prayer, were raised from the dead. These include the son of the widow of Zarephath (1 Kings 17:17-24), the son of the Shunamite woman (2 Kings 4:18-37), and the unnamed man raised from the dead after being placed into Elisha's tomb and touching Elisha's bones (2 Kings 13:21).

In the New Testament, Christ raised the widow's son in the city of Nain (Luke 7:11-17), the daughter of Jarius (Luke 8:40-56), and his friend Lazarus, who had been deceased four days (John 11). In Jerusalem, there was a mass resurrection of many saints when Christ arose (Matt. 27:50-53). Peter raised Dorcus (Acts 9:36-43), and Paul raised Eutychus (Acts 20:7-12). Different circumstances caused each death, but the end result was that each person was raised from the dead by the power of God.

Some of these individuals may have been "revived" from death, while others were "resurrected." When revived, the person has died, but the spirit may have remained in the body for a brief time. In a resurrection, such as the case of Lazarus, the spirit was out of the body and already in the afterworld four days.

After three days in the tomb, Christ was resurrected, as His spirit was three days and nights outside of His body (Matt. 12:40). A resurrection would require that the spirit return from its eternal resting place and reenter the person's body.

The spirits of those who died and were resurrected during the Old Testament era would have returned into the person's body from the subterranean paradise called Abraham's bosom. Before the crucifixion of Christ, when an Old Testament saint died, their spirit descended into the lower parts of the earth. When Old Testament prophets prayed for life to return to the deceased person, God drew their spirits upward, and the spirits returned to their bodies.

In the time of Elijah and Elisha, the two young men they raised from the dead were brought back within a few hours of their announced deaths. But the raising of Lazarus was one of the greatest miracles in Scripture because he was raised on the fourth day. Devout Jews believed that after three days, it was impossible for anybody to be brought back to life. They believed that, by the fourth day of death, the spirit of the departed one had gone to its eternal destination and could not be brought back.

In Matthew 27:50-53, spirits of the saints that rose from the dead and were seen in Jerusalem after Christ's resurrection would have returned from Abraham's bosom and entered back into their bodies. In this instance after Christ's resurrection, each person who rose would have received a body similar to the type of body Christ received at His resurrection. This group of saints resurrected and would not die again. At some point they would have been taken to paradise in the third heaven. These resurrected saints of God were the first fruits of Christ (1 Cor. 15:20), meaning the first saints resurrected among many who would follow in the future resurrection.

A SPIRIT PASSING THROUGH OUTER SPACE

The idea of a human spirit being transported from the earth to the third heaven is intriguing. The Apostle Paul wrote of his own experience of being caught up into the third heaven and seeing paradise. He was uncertain if he was in the body or out of the body (2 Cor. 12:1-4). "In the body" refers to the spirit being in the body while experiencing a full color vision of the heavenly paradise.

An example is John in the book of Revelation. Imprisoned on an island, John described finding himself "in the Spirit." His eyes were opened to see future events from heaven's viewpoint. John would *see*, then write on parchment; he would *hear*, then write. His apocalyptic vision continued for hours, and some scholars believe it may have occurred in succession over a period of many days.

If Paul were "out of the body," his spirit would have been removed temporarily from his physical body. This type of out of body experience happened to my father when he was a young man. He had been praying, fasting, and studying Scripture in a tiny cabin in the mountains of West Virginia. While sitting outside in a chair that he had leaned against the cabin wall, he heard footsteps walking in the leaves.

He turned around and saw a hand reach through the wall of the cabin and touch him on the head. Instantly, his Bible fell on his lap, his head dropped, and his spirit left his body. He looked back and saw himself slumped over and thought he must have died.

Suddenly his spirit took off into the upper atmosphere like a rocket. He traveled quickly through a beautiful expanse of deep blue, as far as his eye could see, until he stopped abruptly and realized he was standing on nothing.

When scientists compile all known available data, they talk about galaxies and solar systems being tens and even hundreds of thousands of light years from the earth. Light travels at 186,000 miles per second. One light year is the distance light travels in one year—nearly six trillion miles. When a Christian has an out-of-body experience, or dies and finds their spirit transported to the third heaven by an angel, how can they arrive in mere moments, when everything outside the earth is billions or trillions of light years away?

In Scripture, we find a couple of men—besides Christ—who were successfully transported alive from the earth to heaven. The first was Enoch, the seventh descendent from Adam. At age sixty-five, Enoch began to walk with God. At age 365, Enoch vanished from the earth, as God translated him to heaven so that he did not see death (Gen. 5:21-24 and Heb. 11:5).

The second person to experience supernatural transition to heaven was Elijah, whose dramatic departure included a whirlwind and a chariot pulled by horses of fire (2 Kings 2:11). A third catching up to heaven occurred when Christ ascended from the Mount of Olives (Acts 1:10-11).

Enoch was translated over 5,000 years ago. Based on the laws that govern light, distance, and speed, by now he might be ascending past Pluto, making the long trek home. Elijah left the earth approximately 2,870 years ago, so cosmic laws indicate he should be passing one of millions of nebulas and some colorful star dust, hoping one day—perhaps in a few million years—to arrive at his destination. In AD 33, when Christ ascended back to the Father from the Mount of Olives, over five hundred believers saw Him go up in a cloud (1 Cor. 15:6). However, considering the number of light years that we are from the third heaven, Christ should still be in that cloud, drifting into the northern section of the cosmic atmosphere, heading toward His heavenly destination.

Yet, months after Christ ascended from the Mount of Olives in Jerusalem (Acts 1:9), Stephen, who was being stoned in Jerusalem, saw the heavens open and Jesus standing at the right hand of God (Acts 7:56). Elijah also successfully arrived at the throne of God. In Zechariah 4:1-14, he is one of two prophets seen in the symbolism of the two olive trees that stand before the throne of God. Elijah will return as one of the two prophets ministering during the tribulation (Mal. 4:5 and Rev. 11:3).

It is a mystery how spirits, including demon spirits, angels, and spirits of departed humans, can move swiftly without being impacted by the physical laws of the cosmic atmosphere. Survival on Earth requires the proper amount of oxygen, gravity, sunlight, and water. If the earth were closer to the sun, heat would consume it; if too far away from the sun, the earth would freeze. For example, Pluto is over four billion miles from planet Earth, and the temperature is around minus 369 degrees Fahrenheit. Human bodies obviously could not travel through that atmosphere and live. So how can a human spirit travel through the galaxies to the third heaven?

PORTALS AND BLACK HOLES

Perhaps the mysterious portals that connect the earthly realm with the heavenly realm hold the answer. Jacob dreamed of seeing a ladder that reached from heaven to earth, with angels ascending and descending the ladder (Gen. 28:12). He called the bottom of the ladder the *house of God*, and the top of the ladder the *gate of heaven*—gate being an entrance, a port, an opening (Gen. 28:17). Rabbis believe the ladder was planted on Mount Moriah, which is the location of the Temple Mount in Jerusalem.

Physicists are still studying a phenomenon called black holes, which are described as the remnants of massive stars that collapsed. A star is a nuclear furnace that burns hydrogen fuel. The force of gravity could crush a star, while the nuclear force tends to blow the star apart. This is a balancing act, and as the star ages and its nuclear fuel is exhausted, the force of gravity causes the star to collapse.

Once the star collapses, no light can escape from the enormous gravitational field. This causes the remains of the star to appear black, and light is forced to orbit around it. Sometimes a black hole is expressed graphically for the audience as fiery light in the shape of a donut, with a black hole in the center of the donut.

Physicists widely agree that many galaxies are powered by an enormous black hole at their center. Our Milky Way galaxy is believed to revolve around a black hole whose mass is three to four million times that of the sun. Some galaxies have black holes that are a thousand times more massive than our own galaxy's black hole.

Albert Einstein gave us a representation of a black hole as two trumpet-like depressions with a funnel connecting them. The funnel was given the name, "the Einstein-Rosen bridge." Einstein thought it was curious that, mathematically, the black hole appears to be a gateway between two entirely different universes. He also speculated that a black hole may open a tunnel in time; in fact, his mathematical equations allow for time travel. Since time and space are related, any bridge that connects two distant regions of space can also connect two different eras of time.

At the center of the funnel called the Einstein-Rosen bridge, gravity become infinite, and the force is so strong that anyone falling into the black hole would be crushed to death and their atoms ripped apart. Even so, the idea of a bridge connecting two different universes has so intrigued theoretical physicists that they believe they may one day send a space probe into a certain section of a black hole and have it come out in a whole different universe—perhaps a parallel universe.

When an angel moves from the earth to the third heaven, gravitational pull is irrelevant. Shifts in gravity, temperature, and oxygen levels do not impact the structure, atoms, and molecules of a spirit. There is no lengthy time travel, as angels move much faster than the speed of light. The same is true with our own spirits. When angels carry our spirits from the earth, we reach our destination in the blink of an eye. From the earth to the third heaven, our spirits will travel at speeds far exceeding the speed of light, even traveling at the speed of thought, which earth's instruments cannot measure.

THE TUNNEL OF DEATH

Among the many near-death experiences that I have heard or read about, there is often a similar thread. When their spirits departed their bodies, people sometimes described the experience as traveling through a long tunnel, usually at great speed. Some say they moved toward a light that appeared small in the distance but increased in color and brightness as they moved closer. Some said the light had personality, as though it could read their thoughts, judge them, and know all about their life on earth. Christians who have had this experience might pass into the light and describe seeing an angel or Christ, or simply being surrounded by the divine presence of the Almighty. When they return, they say that they were brought into a location in heaven.

Others have a near-death experience that seems similar but leads to a different outcome. These describe their spirit leaving their body, but instead of moving upward, they move downward. They go through a tunnel of darkness that might have burning embers along the walls. Descriptions of the encounters at the end of the tunnel vary. Some see complete darkness. Others see glowing fire, including a lake that burns with fire. Some have frightening encounters with people or strange looking creatures. Those with limited biblical knowledge are often frightened when they return, and some seek answers and become followers of Christ. They believe they saw a realm of the afterlife that the Bible calls hell.

Is it possible that the tunnels people say they travel through are the black holes that appear to mathematically connect two universes? Could these black holes play a role in transporting spirits—whether angelic, demonic, or human—between our universe and the third heaven? Nobody can say with certainty unless they receive divine revelation from God, but it is an interesting and plausible theory.

WHEN IS DEATH FINAL?

Scripture teaches that the life of the flesh is in the blood. When the heart stops beating and breathing stops, a person can develop brain damage after ten minutes without oxygen-rich blood flowing through the body. This is one reason resurrection from the dead is such a miracle. The death process should cause permanent damage to the brain and other organs. Yet, those raised by the power of God suffered no serious side-effects.

But when the blood stops flowing, the lungs stop breathing, and the silver cord is severed, the human spirit of a believer leaves the body and returns to God who gave it (Eccl. 12:7).

CHAPTER 3

THE THREE LEVELS OF HEAVEN

One of the Apostle Paul's revelations is that there are three levels of heaven. Without this knowledge, we might think of heaven as being all outer space, or the vast expanse called the cosmic heavens.

Paul taught, "There are celestial bodies, and bodies terrestrial..." (1 Cor. 15:40). Celestial bodies are heavenly, while terrestrial bodies are earthly. Celestial bodies could refer to the sun, moon, planets and stars, but in this context, celestial bodies refer to angelic beings. Celestial would also include those who once lived on the earth, but whose spirits are now in paradise in the third heaven. Paul had a personal experience with the third heaven, which likely happened when he was stoned in Lystra and left for dead.

PAUL'S THIRD HEAVEN ENCOUNTER

In his second epistle to the church at Corinth, Paul alluded to an incident that occurred fourteen years before he wrote of the event. In Acts 14, Paul was being physically threatened. He and his companions fled to Lystra and Derbe, cities in Lycaonia. While ministering, a fantastic healing miracle occurred, causing the heathen people to say, "The gods have come down to us in the likeness of men." Paul rebuked the people for calling them gods. Devout Jews rose up and persuaded the people to stone Paul.

After being pelted with rocks, the angry locals physically dragged Paul outside the city, assuming he was now dead (Acts 14:19). This is likely when he was caught up to the third heaven and saw paradise, the abode where righteous spirits await their resurrection (see 2 Cor. 12:1-4).

This is the only reference in the Bible's sixty-six books that mentions the third heaven. In the beginning God created the heaven and the earth (Gen. 1:1 KJV). The word heaven in the King James translation is singular. After God created for six days, we read, "Thus the heavens and the earth were finished..." (Gen. 2:1).

From that moment forward, the word heaven is written as plural—heavens—one hundred fourteen times throughout the Old Testament. This indicates various levels of heaven.

Scientists tell us that the earth's atmosphere has five distinct layers—troposphere, stratosphere, mesosphere, thermosphere, and exosphere. The troposphere extends five to nine miles above the earth's surface, and the stratosphere extends thirty-one miles above the troposphere. Jets fly in the lower stratosphere because there is less turbulence. I have flown many times when it was cloudy and raining. When the plane moves into the upper stratosphere, the clouds are below us and sunshine is above the storm.

The mesosphere extends about fifty-three miles above the stratosphere, and temperatures grow colder the further you move away from Earth. Here the air is too thin for humans to breathe.

Above the mesosphere is the thermosphere, which is extremely hot—sometimes thousands of degrees. The thermosphere extends 372 miles above the mesosphere, according to the National Aeronautics and Space Administration. The beautiful auroras that can be seen around the polar regions occur in the thermosphere. Satellites operate in this region.

The exosphere is the uppermost layer of the earth's atmosphere. NASA says this layer extends from the top of the thermosphere up to 6,200 miles. The expanse beyond Earth and its atmosphere is outer space, or simply *space*, although scientific boundary definitions of the beginning of outer space vary.

Beyond the earth's atmosphere are vast plains of the universe—stars, planets, the moon, the sun, nebulas, and galaxies. The moon averages a distance of 238,855 miles from the earth, depending on the orbit. The sun is about 93 million miles from the earth, and the closest star, after the sun, is over four light years away. Polaris, also known as the North Star, is 430 light years away from the earth.

This area is accessed by the entire spirit world. Humans could not survive in a physical body in this part of the universe, unless they were wearing a spacesuit that provided oxygen, controlled temperature, and proper air pressure. Only spirits, including the Almighty, angels, demons, and spirits of the deceased, can easily move through the expanse of the second heaven.

In Ephesians chapter six, Paul reveals four types of demonic entities, all working under the authority of Satan himself, that rule in the kingdom of darkness. He mentions principalities, powers, rulers of the darkness of this world, and wicked spirits in high (heavenly) places.

Two biblical examples of principality (prince) spirits are the prince of Persia and the prince of Greece. Both high-level evil spirits were attempting to influence the kings and impact the political affairs of the Persian and Grecian Empires. These spirits were resisting Gabriel, God's angelic messenger, by preventing him from reaching Daniel in Babylon.

The second heaven will become a cosmic war zone during the middle of the great tribulation, as there will be war in heaven between

Michael and his angels and Satan and his angels (Rev. 12:7-10).

If you are in a redemptive covenant with Christ, when you die your spirit will be carried by angels and pass through the first, then the second levels of heaven, where the spirit will find it's home in paradise, located in the third heaven (2 Cor. 12:1-4).

SECTIONS OF PARADISE

The word paradise is used only three times in Scripture. The first time was while Christ was hanging on the cross and He told the dying thief, "Today you shall be with me in paradise" (Luke 23:43). At that time, paradise was a massive chamber prepared under the earth's crust that housed the spirits of the righteous. It was known as Abraham's bosom (Luke 16:22).

The next reference was Paul being caught up to paradise in the third heaven (2 Cor. 12:2-4). The third reference is found in Revelation 2:7, where God promised believers in Ephesus that if they were faithful overcomers, they would eat of the tree of life which is in the midst of the paradise of God.

In all three paradise references, the same Greek word is used which means, "a park, an orchard, a garden, a place of blessedness." The Hebraic pattern of a heavenly paradise is seen in the earthly garden of Eden. In Eden, before the fall of man, there was no sin, sickness, death, fear or pain, and the tree of life was in the center of the garden (Gen. 2:9). Eden would be considered a paradise on earth. It is likely that the Eden on earth was patterned after the garden, trees, flowers, and crystal rivers that existed in heaven at the beginning of creation.

Man is a three-part being—body, soul, and spirit. God is triune— Father, Son, and Holy Spirit. The tabernacle was divided into three sections—outer court, inner court, and Holy of Holies. The cosmic lights are the sun, moon, and stars. Three main Old Testament patriarchs were Abraham, Isaac, and Jacob. The sphere of planet Earth has three levels—crust, mantle, and core (inner and outer). There are three levels of heaven.

I believe that in the heavenly paradise, there are three distinct sections—one for infants, another for children, and another for adults. I base this on the experiences of people who died briefly, saw paradise, but were revived and lived to talk about it.

According to testimonials, the infant section is under the guardianship of angels who teach and care for these little ones. Christ alluded to these angels in Matthew 18:10. This section is for infants who die in the womb or after birth, including those who were miscarried or aborted. Remember, the human spirit is not just breath; it is a living, eternal being. The spirit that is imparted at conception cannot die.

The tiny spirits of the infants mature and grow as they would have on the earth. Eventually they are released into the children's section of paradise.

The children's section is for deceased children from every tribe, nation and ethnic group who passed away during their earthly childhood. Some believers who, through a vision or near-death experience, have observed children in this section of paradise say they appear to be around five through twelve years of age. These children live, learn, and play together, just as children do on earth. There are countless children in heaven—perhaps hundreds of millions. It will be exciting for family members to meet the infants or children that they were unable to spend time with on earth.

The third section is where adults rest until the resurrection. (This is different from the martyr's section under the crystal sea.) Even though there are different sections of paradise, they are all one big city. Think of it as different neighborhoods in the same city. Of course, the children and adults interact with one another, just as they would on earth.

Years ago, in the early hours of the morning, I felt a chest pain and thought I had died. I suddenly found myself in paradise, in heaven. During the experience, I saw two people, one that I knew had died years earlier, and a man that I had not seen in many years. Unbeknown to me at the time, the man had passed away.

I was surrounded by a garden of beautiful flowers in a rainbow of vibrant colors. The trees were enormous. I saw modern cities with stunning and unusual buildings that appeared to be made of precious gemstones. In another section to my right and away from the city were massive marble buildings, similar to the ancient structures in Greece and Rome. The sound of people singing and worshipping was coming from these large structures. I had the impression that people lived in sections of paradise where the land and architecture were reminiscent of their time on earth.

One thing that caught my eye was a round, open air arena where children from different nations were gathered to sing and worship. I saw only one adult among them. Her name was Tracy Davis, and she had been my wife's best friend who died in a car accident. She was directing the worship.

In this area I saw small hills upon which tiny houses were built, much like a playhouse you might build for a child. The houses in this area had the same design style that reminded me of the homes I had seen in Romania. They were cute little dwellings, all the same color. It was as though each child had their own place where they could invite other children to come over and play.

ANIMALS IN PARADISE

People have debated the existence of animals in heaven, and specifically, they want to know if their pets will be there. We find no Scripture to confirm or deny that pets go to heaven. In biblical times, we don't read of people having animals as pets, as the animals that people owned in

Scripture were typically used for work, food, and sacrifice (under the old covenant).

We know there are animals in heaven because the Bible mentions white horses that the armies of heaven will ride when they return to the earth to rule with Christ (Rev. 19:14).

God created birds, sea creatures, cattle, and beasts of the earth before He created Adam. It was Adam who named the animals: "And Adam gave names to all cattle, and to the fowl of the air, and to every beast of the field; but for Adam there was not found a help meet for him" (Gen. 2:20). Notice that Eve had not been created. Outside of God, the only companionship Adam had at first was the many animals that lived with him in Eden.

In Genesis 3, we read that the serpent was crafty, more so than any beast of the field that God created. Moses wrote that the serpent carried on a conversation with Eve. Most people laugh at this or believe it is a myth, since animals and snakes cannot talk.

However, the Jewish historian Josephus wrote that before Adam and Eve sinned, the serpent had the power of speech. After the temptation and sin, God took away the serpent's voice and placed poison in its mouth. Presently, animals can communicate among their own kind. It may be possible that, before the fall of Adam, he was given the ability to communicate with animals. Some animals can still speak; for instance, talking birds. We have an African grey that mimics the speech of family members. When I enter the front door of our house, she hears my voice and begins to make whistles and sounds.

As with Adam in the beginning of his life, many people today have no earthly companion and no family living close by. One of their greatest comforts is their pets, usually dogs or cats. To many people, pets are family. These loving pets fill a void of loneliness by giving their owners unconditional love, attention, and affection.

When we arrive in our heavenly home, there will be no loneliness, isolation, depression, or lack. It is difficult for earthly minds to comprehend the perfection of heaven. The atmosphere is permeated with perfect love. Generations of covenant followers from all nations will merge into one family of God, lacking nothing and dwelling with joy and perfect peace.

The creation of animals was not a new idea to God. We can assume that animals exist in heaven because God created them on the earth in the beginning. The prototypes of things God created on earth exist in heaven, and that would include animals. God's creations that bring joy, companionship, or comfort to a person on earth are surely found in heaven.

When considering the perfection of heaven, I am reminded of this verse, "No good thing will He withhold from those who walk uprightly" (Psa. 84:11). I believe we will be speechless when we see the stunning beauty of the landscape—the multi-colored flowers, grassy fields, crystal sea, enormous trees—and the fruit, vegetation, and animals that we will find in paradise.

CHAPTER 4

THE PARADISE WHERE MARTYRS ARE RESTING

The man was a Christian and the Bishop of Smyrna, one of the seven churches mentioned in Revelation (Rev. 2:8). Jerome, an early church father, said this man was a disciple of the Apostle John, who had ordained the man and placed him over Smyrna. He was considered one of the top three apostolic church fathers, which included Clement and Ignatius. He was bound and burned at the stake, and when the fire did not consume his body, he was stabbed. His name was Polycarp, one of the early martyrs of the faith.

In the Christian faith, a martyr is a person whose life is taken because of their religious beliefs. Often, the slaying of a Christian occurs at the hands of those with an opposing religious belief, especially those who consider the spread of Christianity a threat that might lead to conversions. In the New Testament, the Pharisees were highly protective of the laws in the Torah, as well as their man-made traditions. Any opposing teaching was called heresy and the alleged false teacher was worthy of death. Paul, a former Pharisee, stayed on the Pharisee hit list and eventually was beheaded in Rome.

Christian sources estimate that seventy million believers have been martyred since the time of Christ. These numbers include Christians exterminated by the Chinese during the Boxer Rebellion, by Mao Zedong during China's Cultural Revolution, by the Turkish Muslims during the Massacre of Armenian Christians, by Communists who took over Russia in 1917, and by Germany's Nazi party. Before that, Christians were persecuted and martyred under ten Roman emperors, beginning with Nero in the year 54 and ending with Diocletian two and a half centuries later. By the 12th century, the church in Rome began to persecute Christians who opposed the false doctrines and traditions that had increasingly crept into the church.

These martyrs will be raised when Christ returns. Paul taught that when the trumpet of God sounds, the dead in Christ shall rise first (1 Thess. 4:16). All Christians who were slain for the Gospel after the birth of the church and during the church age now inhabit the martyrs' paradise.

According to John, another group of martyrs will be slain *during* the great tribulation. These are people who will be executed by beheading because they refused to receive the mark of the beast or worship his image (see Rev. 20:4). The word *beheaded* is used five times in the New Testament, four of which are in reference to John the Baptist, where it means "to decapitate." However, in Revelation 20:4, a different Greek word is used that places an emphasis on the weapon—an ax—used as the tool used to behead a person. Tribulation martyrs will die a very violent death for remaining faithful to Christ and for refusing to follow the antichrist.

THE MARTYR'S PARADISE

The book of Revelation indicates that there is a specific location in heaven where the souls of martyrs dwell. The Apostle John wrote of immediately being *caught up* to the throne room of God (Rev. 4:1-2).

The floor of God's throne room is massive, to the point that tens of millions of souls can stand before God at one time.

Situated close to God's throne is a sacred piece of furniture identified as the golden altar where incense is offered up to God, mingled with the prayers of the saints (Rev. 8:3-4). John described the floor as a sea of glass, like crystal, which would have allowed John to see the martyred souls that were underneath the altar. John wrote:

> "When He opened the fifth seal, I saw under the altar the souls of those who had been slain for the word of God and for the testimony which they held. And they cried with a loud voice, saying, 'How long, O Lord, holy and true, until You judge and avenge our blood on those who dwell on the earth?' Then a white robe was given to each of them; and it was said to them that they should rest a little while longer, until both the number of their fellow servants and their brethren, who would be killed as they were, was completed."
>
> — Revelation 6:9-11

The Greek word slain is *sphazo*, and it refers to a violent death. It is used when describing an animal that is being butchered, or one slain to be offered for a sacrifice. These are the souls of people who lived on earth and laid down their lives as the ultimate sacrifice. When their souls departed their bodies on earth, they each would have been carried by angels to the third heaven and placed in this beautiful location, under the watchful eye of God Himself.

In this paradise, each martyr is given a white robe. It is possible these robes are placed upon them the moment their spirits exit their body, prior to entering this martyr's paradise. Later in Revelation, we read that many of these martyrs were beheaded for the word of God and for their testimony (Rev. 20:4).

Under the decree of the cruel Roman emperor Nero, the Apostle Paul himself faced a violent death by beheading. Paul wrote his final letter, revealing that there was a crown of righteousness laid up for him (2 Tim. 4:8). *Laid up* means that it is reserved and waiting.

A crown of righteousness is one of five different crowns an overcomer could receive at the Judgment Seat of Christ. James wrote that when a person endures testing, he shall receive a crown of life (James 1:12). Christ warned the church at Smyrna that they would be persecuted, tested, and cast into prison. He promised them, "Be faithful unto death, and I will give you a crown of life" (Rev. 2:10). I believe this crown of life is the reward for those who walked in the Spirit, disciplined their flesh during trials and hardships, endured persecution, or accepted martyrdom for the Word of God and their testimony in Christ. Paul knew that he had a crown of righteousness waiting for him, and he also had a crown of life.

In this unique martyrs' section, once a soul arrives, they are told to rest for a season. This common Greek word *rest* refers to "take ease; refresh." In the book of Hebrews, the writer speaks of how, through unbelief, Israel failed to enter into rest (Heb. 3:18-19). The writer then wrote, "There remains therefore a rest for the people of God" (Heb. 4:9). This word *rest* in Greek refers to the uninterrupted rest we enter into when we are caught up to meet the Lord at His return (1 Thess. 4:16-17), or when we are resurrected at Christ's return (1 Cor. 15:52).

THE BIG HEAVENLY SABBATICAL

What about our family and friends who have died in Christ and their bodies buried? Even though their corruptible bodies are in the grave, their souls and spirits are very much alive and resting in paradise in the third heaven, where they await our arrival (2 Cor. 12:4). They have "ceased from their (earthly) works" (Heb. 4:10).

One of the sin curses brought upon Adam and his descendants is that man would till the ground by the sweat of his brow, as the ground now would be cursed with thorns and thistles (Gen. 3:17-19). Ceasing from labor would allude to no longer having to work to pay bills or sweat and grow tired from hard labor. One of the Greek words translated as rest in the book of Hebrews is the Greek word *sabbatismos*, which refers to a Sabbath, or a rest.

In the Torah (the first five books of the Old Testament), after six days of speaking life and creating, God rested on the seventh day (Gen. 2:2). One day of rest at the conclusion of every week became an established rule among the Hebrew people and was one of the Ten Commandments: "Remember the Sabbath day, to keep it holy" (Exod. 20:8). On the Jewish calendar, the seventh day (Saturday) was set aside as a day in which people were to refrain from all labor. This also provided animals a day of rest.

Death is a release from earthly labor and an entering into an *eternal Sabbath of rest*, awaiting the resurrection and the future millennial kingdom on earth.

Do not view rest with a Western mindset, which is to lie down on the couch and take a nap, or to sit back lazily in a recliner. The sabbatical rest of souls of the deceased in Christ does not mean sitting down and doing nothing or floating on a cloud while angels play harps. The departed souls are involved with activities they enjoy, without the sweat and toil of earthly labor. Rest includes fellowshipping with others, worshipping, eating, and becoming acquainted with other saints throughout the ages.

Imagine meeting Noah and discussing how he and his sons cut trees and built the ark over a one-hundred-year period, and learning from him other details not written in the Bible. When you die and enter paradise, you can meet those who are mentioned in the "great cloud of witnesses" in Hebrews 11-12, including Abraham, Isaac, Jacob, Joseph, Daniel, David, the sons of Jacob, the apostles of Christ, Paul and others.

As a child sitting in Sunday School or listening to my father and others preach or talk about heaven, my first impression was that this was a place where old church people go when they die. My young friends never mentioned heaven, as it was an obscure and distant land, somewhere far beyond the sun. It seemed that every other song that was sung by the elder generation talked about dying, going to heaven, and hanging out with someone there, especially Jesus or your mother.

In my young mind, I was not interested in the place, as I imagined it must be boring, with no games or toys. I was somewhat fascinated by streets of gold and gates of pearl and how much they must be worth in cash. I was curious about who mined all the gold and how big the oyster was that formed a gate from one pearl. These were thoughts from the mind of a child with an overactive imagination.

For most people in the church, heaven becomes more appealing after family and close friends leave their earthly home and take the journey billions of light years away, to the land of the beginning, as it is written, "In the beginning, God created the heaven and the earth" (Gen. 1:1 KJV). As weeks turn to months, months to years, and the years add up to decades, the older we grow, the closer we come to crossing the line from mortality to immortality and thinking about eternity and our heavenly home.

HEAVEN'S HONOR ROLL

In the early church, if you converted to Christ and were added to the church (Acts 2:47), there was a strong possibility you would experience persecution. Other religions and the leaders in Judea and Rome viewed Christianity as a new cult that presented a new deity. Devout Jews saw Christianity as a threat, as many Jews were becoming believers, accepting that Christ was the promised Messiah. If you were an apostolic leader in the early church, jail time would likely be on your itinerary, or you could be arrested and end up on the honor roll of heaven as a martyr.

Of the original apostles, with Matthias taking the place of Judas, eleven were martyrs who were slain by methods such as beheading, stoning, piercing with the sword, or crucifixion. John was the only apostle to escape dying a martyr, although he came close. History and church tradition teach:

- Andrew preached in Asia Minor (Turkey and Greece) and died by crucifixion.

- Thomas journeyed to India, where he was pierced through with the spears of four soldiers and thrown into a flaming oven.

- Philip, after winning to Christ the wife of a noted Roman proconsul, was beaten, imprisoned, and crucified.

- Matthew was believed, by tradition, to have been beheaded in Ethiopia.

- Bartholomew traveled to several countries to preach and was beaten and crucified.

- James, the brother of John, was beheaded.

- James, the brother of Jesus, was stoned and clubbed to death.

- Simon the Zealot preached in Persia and was killed for refusing to sacrifice to a sun god.

- Matthias replaced Judas, and while not much is known about him, it is believed that he was stoned and beheaded in Jerusalem.

- Peter was crucified in an upside-down position.

- Jude was also crucified at Edessa.

According to church history, under the order of Emperor Domitian, John was lowered into a large vessel of boiling oil, but it did not harm him. Through God's protection, he survived and was banished to the island of Patmos, where he experienced the vision of the Apocalypse. After Domitian's death, John was released. He copied by hand his series of visions and died around the age of one hundred.

Stephen was the first martyr mentioned in the Bible, having been stoned outside of Jerusalem with the consent of Saul of Tarsus, who later converted to Christ and became the Apostle Paul.

At Paul's conversion, Christ told him that he would suffer many things for the sake of following Christ (Acts 9:16). On numerous occasions Paul encountered close calls with death. He was stoned, dragged outside the city of Lystra, and left for dead (Acts 14:19). Before following Christ, he had slain church leaders. At the conclusion of his ministry, he was beheaded in Rome and would be added to the honor roll of heaven as a martyr.

Christ sent a message to the church at Pergamos, a city called "the seat of Satan." Christ mentioned an early martyr named Antipas, who was a faithful servant in the church (Rev. 2:13). This man was part of a Christian community that had held fast to the name of the Lord and had not denied the faith. Antipas is the *only name* of a righteous person mentioned in the messages to the seven churches.

When Stephen was being persecuted before he was stoned, he saw a vision of Jesus standing at the right hand of God (Acts 7:55). It is believed that Christ was preparing to personally receive and welcome Stephen's spirit to heaven, as Stephen's final prayer was, "Lord Jesus, receive my spirit" (Acts 7:59). After this prayer, Stephen kneeled down and "fell asleep" (Acts 7:60). Falling asleep is a biblical euphemism for dying. These two verses indicate that, at death, the spirit of the individual is received in heaven and Christ knows the person is arriving.

THE TEMPLE OF THE TABERNACLE OF THE TESTIMONY

The throne room and the martyr's paradise located under the crystal floor are just two regions of the third heaven. Revelation 15:5 tells us, "And after this I looked and the temple of the tabernacle of the testimony in heaven was opened." The word *tabernacle* is first mentioned in Scripture when Moses built a tabernacle in the wilderness. This was a portable traveling tent that could be set up, taken down, and reset at different locations. Inside this rectangular animal skin compound was sacred wooden furniture overlaid in bronze and gold.

The pattern for creating this furniture was based upon a vision Moses experienced of the same sacred furniture in the heavenly temple. The temple in heaven includes the ark of the covenant (Rev. 11:19), a golden altar (Rev. 8:3), and a seven-branched golden candelabra, positioned near the throne of God (Rev. 1:20). In Revelation 15:5, John used the Greek word *skene*, translated as *temple*, which refers to a cloth tent or hut, but can also allude to a divine habitation. This heavenly temple is God's divine habitation.

John identified God's throne room as the *temple* or the *temple in heaven* multiple times in the book of Revelation. The temple in Jerusalem was a solid stone structure, built with white Jerusalem limestone that was skillfully cut by stone cutters. The temple's outer court compound and the building itself became the permanent home for six pieces of holy furniture, all used during the daily or yearly rituals of the priests, which included praying, offering sacrifices, and presenting offerings.

From Scripture, we understand that God's original ark of the covenant is in heaven, behind the throne of God. In Revelation 11:19, the doors of the temple opened, and John could see the ancient ark of the covenant inside.

The prophet Isaiah also saw the inside of this temple in a vison (Isa. 6:1-6). He spoke of the back of God's robe (called a "train") filling the temple, as seraphim cried out, "Holy, holy, holy is the Lord of hosts."

I personally believe that the entrance into all other parts of heaven, including access to the holy city New Jerusalem, could be through the massive doors of this heavenly temple. This would mean that a person could not enter the celestial city without first worshiping God on His throne, then entering the doors that lead through the temple into other parts of heaven.

This heavenly temple of the tabernacle of the testimony presently houses the tribulation bowl judgments (see Revelation 16) and the seven trumpets that will be blown by the seven angels during the seven-year tribulation (Rev. 8-9). Each separate trumpet blast unleashes a cataclysmic judgment on the earth. This temple becomes the center of all worship, judgments, and future apocalyptic activity.

The phrase *"the temple of the tabernacle of the testimony"* is interesting. The word testimony is the Greek word *martyrion,* from a root word *martus,* which alludes to *a witness.* In Revelation 15:5, the word testimony gives a stunning clue to the purpose of this heavenly tabernacle of the testimony, as the word witness is related to evidence. This facility appears to house some type of evidence.

At the Judgment Seat of Christ and the Great White Throne Judgment, books will be opened. John noted that at the judgments, the books were opened. This included the Book of Life. John added that "the dead were judged out of those things which were written in the books, according to their works" (Rev. 20:12). I believe this temple of the testimony houses the information that has been recorded by angels, perhaps even a person's guardian angel, that reveals their words and works.

Those with a redemptive covenant have their names written in the Lamb's Book of Life, which is the official registry of heaven. Christ told seventy of His disciples to "rejoice because your names are written in heaven" (Luke 10:20). This also indicates that the recording rooms where information is inscribed are likely within this tabernacle of the testimony of the covenant.

OTHER UNUSUAL BOOKS IN HEAVEN

Many years ago, when my father was first called into the ministry, he had a strange experience that he related many times over the years. In a night vision, the Spirit of the Lord brought him to a specific building that was located somewhere in heaven. He went inside and observed what appeared to be a massive library filled with books. These were not normal sized books, but they were so large that it took both hands to pick up one of them and remove it from a shelf. It also took both hands to turn the pages.

He saw titles on the spines of the books, including a two-volume set titled, "The Prophecies of Jesus." He started to reach for the first volume when he heard a voice say, "That one is not for you." He then noted on the shelf several large books with the title, "The Mighty Acts and Words of Jesus." He retrieved one of those heavy books and laid it on a beautiful table. He was amazed to see that the book contained pictures of all the miracles recorded in the Bible, and even some that were not recorded in Scripture, along with an explanation of the event. Pictures filled in the blanks of the Bible stories, giving minute details of miracles Jesus performed on earth (John 21:25). Dad did not know how the images were captured for this volume, but he said it was as though a photographer followed Jesus, took pictures, and documented each event. The images were clear and detailed. One image showed how Jesus anointed the hands of His disciples and sent them throughout a large, outdoor crowd, laying hands upon the people to receive healing. Other photos showed lines of children waiting for Christ to bless them.

Before Dad's death, he told me that he believed the book of prophecies was not for him, but that it had been set aside in this season for me to preach, teach, and explain the prophecies of Christ from Scripture.

ANGELS KEEP RECORDS

For centuries it has been believed that specific angels are assigned as scribes to keep records at the heavenly temple. For a name to be inscribed in, or blotted out of, the Book of Life, reasoning would indicate there are angels assigned to inscribe or remove names at the temple of the testimony in heaven.

Christ indicated that there is joy in the presence of the angels of God over one sinner who repents (Luke 15:10). Clearly, angels are aware when a sinner on earth repents. Is an announcement made in the celestial temple? Are the souls and spirits of the departed who are resting in paradise in the third heaven made aware when a close loved one repents (2 Cor. 12:1-4)?

God's record keeping system is flawless. The psalmist said that God counts the number of the stars and calls them all by their names (Psa. 147:4). There are said to be about 100 billion stars in our galaxy, and perhaps the same number in other galaxies. The Bible mentions Arcturus, Orion, and Pleiades (Job 9:9). God, who created all, knows all. Yet, He also notices the smallest things, such as when a sparrow falls to the ground (Matt. 10:29).

Each martyr is known. All idle words and works of men are recorded. On the Day of Judgment, books will be opened, and people will give an account of everything written in the books (Matt. 16:27).

When considering eternity, remember this. It is not the things that people are saying about you on earth that matter for eternity. It is what heaven is saying about you. It is not your name that carries weight, but the fact that your name is inscribed in the Lamb's Book of Life. It doesn't matter who you know in this life. The eternal issue is, do you personally know and have favor with the Judge who is sitting on His throne?

CHAPTER 5

YOUR NEXT BODY YOU'VE ALWAYS WANTED

Years ago, when my father passed away, the family went to the funeral home for a brief viewing. Mom looked at the handsome, white-haired shell of her husband of fifty-six years and said, "He looks so good, if he'd get up, I'd marry him all over again."

Sometime later, I asked a funeral home director a question. After the hundreds of people whom they have laid to rest over the years, I wanted to know if he could tell the difference between someone who died a Christian and someone who did not. He immediately commented, "Yes, I can. One of the differences is the level of sorrow versus the level of peace. Everyone grieves. It's a normal human process. However, peace is visible on the faces of those who are Christians and know that their loved one was spiritually prepared to meet the Lord. The funerals of those I knew who were wicked in their life and had no spiritual upbringing are permeated with sorrow and sadness. It's the difference between hope and hopelessness."

There is no fear of death for those who are in Christ Jesus. Several times I have told the story of the months before my dad passed away at a care facility in Cleveland, Tennessee. He had suffered from diabetes for years and was on dialysis because of kidney failure. His body seemed to be weakening by the day.

Sitting in the car in the driveway of his house, I asked him what it feels like, knowing that he soon will pass from this life to the next, and what does he think the experience will be like?

He noted that for him, there was no fear in dying, as he understood the process of departing this life from the perspective of the inspired Word of God. He viewed the process as a transfer from one location to another. He thought for a moment when I asked what he thought the moment of departure would be like. He answered, "I think it will be glorious!"

In Hebrews 2:14-15, we read these powerful words: "Inasmuch then as the children have partaken of flesh and blood, He Himself likewise shared in the same, that through death He might destroy him who had the power of death, that is, the devil, and release those who through fear of death were all their lifetime subject to bondage."

The death and resurrection of Christ was a demonstration of the process that, up until that time, people were unfamiliar with. Throughout the Old Testament, there was not a great spiritual revelation on death and resurrection. Elisha raised a woman's son from the dead (2 Kings 4), and a dead man came back to life when his corpse was placed in Elisha's tomb (2 Kings 13:21). In neither case are there any testimonies or commentaries that tell us where their spirits had been before they were raised, or what they saw in the afterlife. The emphasis in both narratives is the supernatural resurrection, and not a question of what the people saw when they arrived at their destination after they died.

In the case of Christ, we know about His pre-death experiences, crucifixion, and resurrection because writers documented those details in Scripture. The Apostle Paul wrote accounts of the three days and nights that Christ spent in the heart of the earth, and he wrote about the resurrection (1 Cor. 15). We also understand the supernatural abilities of a person in a resurrected body. For a follower of Christ, the fear of death has been removed.

FROM THE CROSS TO THE THRONE

The death process for Christ began at the cross. He already had lost blood when He was scourged at the whipping post and pierced with nails in His hands and feet. It was the slow, painful execution by crucifixion and the loss of blood that finally took His life. When the centurion pierced Christ's side, blood and water flowed from His heart, which symbolically could represent salvation through the blood of Christ and the water of baptism that allows us to enter a redemptive covenant with Him.

Mark 15:37 (KJV) says that Christ "gave up the ghost." The word *ghost* is the old English word once used to describe a spirit. In this case it speaks of the spirit of Christ that left His earthly body and was taken to the underground chamber of the righteous souls (Abraham's bosom).

We know this is what occurred because Christ predicted: "For as Jonah was three days and three nights in the belly of the great fish, so will the Son of Man be three days and three nights in the heart of the earth" (Matt. 12:40-41 NKJV)

A wealthy, secret follower of Jesus named Joseph of Arimathea asked Pilate for the lifeless, blood covered body of Christ. Joseph obtained one hundred pounds of linens and spices for wrapping the corpse of Christ; then he laid Christ's body in his own cavernous tomb carved into solid limestone. A round, heavy stone covered the entrance, and then was sealed with a Roman seal to keep anyone from entering (Matt. 27:64). The Pharisees feared that the disciples were secretly plotting to steal the body and falsely announce that their Messiah had risen from the dead.

As His body lay wrapped like a mummy on a stone slab in the dark, cool limestone tomb, Christ's spirit was very much alive in the subterranean world where the spirits of the righteous were confined, somewhere in the heart of the earth (Matt. 12:40).

This was the great underground gathering place of Abraham, Isaac, Jacob, the sons of Jacob, all the Hebrew prophets, and all the people of faith from previous centuries. Christ had a special three-day assignment while His spirit was joined with these righteous patriarchs. We read:

> "Wherefore he saith, when he ascended up on high, he led captivity captive, and gave gifts unto men. (Now that he ascended, what is it but that he also descended first into the lower parts of the earth? He that descended is the same also that ascended up far above all heavens, that he might fill all things.)"
>
> — Ephesians 4:8-10 (KJV)

Peter also noted Christ's ministry activity after His spirit descended into the lower parts (heart) of the earth:

> "For Christ also hath once suffered for sins, the just for the unjust, that he might bring us to God, being put to death in the flesh, but quickened by the Spirit: By which also he went and preached unto the spirits in prison."
>
> — 1 Peter 3:18-19 (KJV)

DEAD SAINTS AROSE

Peter was referring to Christ's three days under the earth. Notice that Christ preached to the spirits that were confined in this place, which was more like an underground prison, as they could not leave and had no access to heaven until after Christ arose.

On the first day of the week, when Christ was raised from the dead, something spectacular occurred. One Gospel writer reported on the event:

> *"And the graves were opened; and many bodies of the saints which slept arose, and came out of the graves after his resurrection, and went into the holy city, and appeared unto many."*
>
> – MATTHEW 27:52-53 (KJV)

Why did the bodies of these saints rise from the dead? Christ preached to their spirits, and then the spirit of Christ came out of the underworld of the righteous and entered back into His body. He then was able to release all the spirits of righteous men and women who had died, including under the old covenant, as far back as the beginning of human time.

This stunning reference in Matthew implies that those who arose and appeared to many in Jerusalem were individuals who may have died *during* the ministry of Jesus and were recognized by those who knew them. Most church fathers quote and confirm this passage, indicating that many saints arose when Christ arose. This miraculous event occurred to prove that Christ was the Messiah and that He truly is *the resurrection and the life* (John 11:25).

What eventually happened to those saints who were resurrected from the grave with Christ? Since these people had already died and their bodies were in the grave, they cannot die again. Thus, the souls who were raised were, at some point, taken to heaven and are presently in paradise. We are uncertain if they were taken into paradise when Christ told Mary that He must ascend, or forty days later when Christ was taken up in a cloud. We do know that they would not have remained on earth in a resurrected body, or else they would still be with us.

When Thomas later saw Christ, at first he thought that he was seeing the spirit of Christ or an apparition of Christ. Jesus reminded Thomas that a spirit does not have flesh and bones, which Christ had when He appeared to Thomas (Luke 24:39).

Peter noted that Christ's soul was not left in hell (the underworld), neither did His flesh see corruption (decay), but He arose with His body completely intact (Acts 2:27-32). Because the body of Christ was entombed with no blood and was tightly wrapped in linen and spices, His body was preserved during the three days. Even the scars in His hands, feet, and side were preserved, which we know because Thomas could see and physically touch the wounds on Christ's body (John 20:27). The scars were necessary to prove this was Christ and not an imposter.

Christ will bear these scars for eternity. He is a marked covenant man, able to prove that He is the mediator of the new covenant. In the future one-thousand-year rule of Christ on earth, these five wounds will still be on Christ, as indicated by the Prophet Zechariah. When the Messiah (Christ) returns to Israel in the millennial reign, He will be questioned about His wounds: "And one shall say unto him, What are these wounds in thine hands? Then he shall answer, those with which I was wounded in the house of my friends" (Zechariah 13:6 KJV).

FOUR THINGS A RESURRECTED BODY CAN DO

After Christ's resurrection, there were four astonishing things He could do that He was unable to do in an earthly body, prior to His resurrection. At our resurrection, we shall be like Him (1 John 3:2). Our new body will have the same abilities that Christ demonstrated during the forty days that He was seen alive after the resurrection. These demonstrations are called *infallible proofs* (Acts 1:3).

1. Walk through solid objects (John 20:19)

A physical earthly body cannot pass through a solid object. Several hours after Mary spoke with Christ at the tomb, He appeared to His frightened disciples, who were huddled together in a room with the doors and windows locked. Christ, who was on the outside of the house, suddenly appeared inside the room in their midst, to the shock of the men (John 20:19). He used a metaphor, saying, "I am the door" (John 10:9). As the door of life, He controls your entrance into the world and your exit from the world. He told the church of Philadelphia that He has the key (authority) to open doors that nobody can shut, and close doors that nobody can open (Rev. 3:7).

After the resurrection, Christ stated that His body was flesh and bone (Luke 24:39) which, in that form, should not be able to pass through a solid wall or door. The only explanation is that a resurrected body has the ability to bypass human restrictions and transport through solid objects.

2. Appear, then suddenly disappear

Mary arrived at Christ's tomb early in the morning on the first day of the week. She did not recognize Him until she heard His voice. He said: "Touch me not; for I am not yet ascended to my Father: but go to my brethren, and say unto them, I ascend unto my Father, and your Father; and to my God, and your God" (John 20:17 KJV).

The phrase "touch me not" might allude to the fact that once a year on the Day of Atonement, when the High Priest was ministering in the Holy of Holies, no one was permitted to touch him physically due to the law of sanctification and defilement. According to *W. E. Vines Greek Dictionary*, the phrase can read, "Do not cling to me."

Christ was saying, "I am preparing now to ascend to my Father, so do not delay me right now." His purpose for ascending was to cleanse the articles in the heavenly temple, and thus fulfill the pattern in the Torah that required a spotless lamb to be presented to God at the temple. Christ was the Lamb, and He had to present himself to God in heaven, as He provided eternal redemption for all who believe.

Between the time He spoke to Mary and the time He appeared in the home to His disciples, Jesus made a sudden appearance at the temple in heaven. He had to present His blood and purify the things in heaven, because this was the place where, in ages past, Satan and a third of the angels transgressed in an attempted coup, thereby defiling the temple with rebellion. Christ presented His blood, became the new High Priest, and provided all righteous souls access at death to enter the heavenly paradise. From that moment forward, no soul of a born-again believer ever descends into Abraham's bosom. They are all taken up to the paradise in heaven.

The unusual ability to appear, disappear, and reappear is evident in the story of the man on the road to Emmaus. Christ was walking on the road to Emmaus, explaining the Scripture from the Law and the Prophets concerning the Messiah. Suddenly, when the eyes of the two men opened to recognize Christ, He vanished from their sight (Luke 24:13-30). Literally, He disappeared out of their sight. This will occur at Christ's return when the living will be changed in a moment, in the twinkling of an eye (1 Cor. 15:51). We will be visible one moment, then suddenly changed from mortal to immortal, and vanish from sight as we are caught up to meet the Lord in the air (1 Thess. 4:17). The phrase *caught up* in Greek is *harpazo*. It refers to being snatched out suddenly, as if to grab someone and physically force them out of danger.

A resurrected body can appear, then suddenly be transported at the speed of thought to another location. I have told youth groups that when you have a resurrected body, there are two things you will not do. One is play "hide and seek." By the time you find their hiding place, the person can think themselves to another location. This could go on endlessly. The other is running a race. Let's say you want to run the length of the New Jerusalem, which is 1,500 miles. By the time the resurrected runners line up and are given the word to go, they can be at the finish line, because they can move as fast as they can think.

This may seem strange or impossible, but there is no other explanation for how Christ could be walking on a road, then appear in a house, then appear in Galilee unless He had been supernaturally transported. The distance between Jerusalem and the Sea of Galilee is approximately a hundred miles. Imagine how long it would take to walk that distance. However, a resurrected body is eternal, so no time constraints are placed on it; therefore, distance and time become irrelevant.

An angel can be in heaven one moment, seconds later be on an earthly assignment, then hours later report back to heaven. Christ ascended to heaven, and weeks later Stephen saw Him standing at the right hand of God (Acts 7:56). Clearly, Christ was able to travel without limitations, in the same manner as angels. Even the speed of light has limitations. Yet, our prayers from the earth can reach heaven the same day (see Dan. 10:12).

3. You will eat in a resurrected body (Luke 24:41)

Some people assume that people in a resurrected body never eat. If this were true, why will the followers of Christ be present in heaven at the Marriage Supper of the Lamb? Also, there is a tree of life that yields twelve different fruits each month, which are used as food (Rev. 22:2, 14).

Another point is that the manna provided to the Israelites in the wilderness for forty years was called "bread from heaven" and "angel's food" (Exod. 16:4; Psa. 78:25). This food originated in heaven and was delivered to the Hebrew people at night, where it was collected from the ground and eaten to sustain the nation. In Genesis 18, the Lord and two angels (who appeared as men) ate bread, meat, and cheese that Sarah and Abraham provided for them.

After His resurrection, Christ enjoyed a meal of fresh fish caught with His disciples at the Sea of Galilee (John 21:12). Christ told His disciples that He will eat with them in the future kingdom (Matt. 26:29).

There are a few mysteries surrounding a resurrected body. I once was asked to answer children's questions about heaven. Two of the questions were: "When we eat in heaven, will we go to the bathroom the way we do now?" Another was, "Will I have a gold commode in my mansion?" The child assumed that if we walk on streets of transparent gold (Rev. 21:21), then why wouldn't the toilet seat in heaven be made of gold?

On the earth, food is necessary for nourishment for our bodies. Adam ate from the tree of life while in a physical body, and the power of the fruit kept him alive. According to Genesis 3:22, eating from the tree of life would have allowed Adam to live forever. That same tree is in heaven and will produce similar results for all who eat from it.

We all will eat in heaven, as well as on the earth during the thousand-year reign of Christ and in the city of New Jerusalem.

4. Christ was seen and touched by those who loved Him (Luke 24:39)

An angel, demon, or spirit coming out of the body at death typically cannot be seen by people who are alive. However, our flesh sometimes can *sense* when a spirit is present. An angel from the Lord might bring a holy hush or reverence in a room. A demonic spirit creates an uncomfortable presence, fear, or chaos. When the spirit of a follower of Christ is leaving its earthly body, the room is suddenly peaceful and might have a feeling of electricity that will cause the hair to stand up on our arms. Once out of the body, the spirit of the deceased can see other spirits, including angels, Christ, God, and the spirits of loved ones who are in paradise.

When Christ arose from the dead, His followers could touch Him, as indicated when Thomas felt Christ's hands and the wound in His side. When I think about seeing my dearest loved ones or close friends who have gone to be with the Lord, it would be sad if we could see them in heaven only as three-dimensional holograms and never hug them. Heaven would not be complete if we existed only as ghostly images that could communicate.

I am aware that in the resurrection we neither marry nor are given in marriage (Matt. 22:30). However, I deeply love my wife of over forty-one years, and I imagine that one day she and I will walk through a beautiful section of heaven, holding hands and talking with Jesus and the patriarchs, fellowshipping with our children and family members, or just enjoying the beauty that God created for His children. The thought of seeing our close friends and loved ones again and spending eternity with them is the greatest comfort to a believer. As the Apostle Paul wrote:

> *"For if the dead rise not, then is not Christ raised: And if Christ be not raised, your faith is vain; ye are yet in your sins. Then they also which are fallen asleep in Christ are perished. If in this life only we have hope in Christ, we are of all men most miserable.*
>
> *– 1 Corinthians 15:16-19 (KJV)*

We as believers have much to look forward to, and we will be amazed at how much God has hidden from us that will surprise us. Paul saw paradise and said that he heard things that it was unlawful (not permissible) to tell (2 Cor. 12:4). He also wrote that "eye has not seen, nor ear heard, the things that God has prepared for them that love Him" (1 Cor. 2:9).

MEETING THE HEROES OF FAITH

Christ made another exciting promise that is recorded in Matthew 8:11: "And I say to you that many will come from east and west, and sit down with Abraham, Isaac, and Jacob in the kingdom of heaven."

God made a covenant with Abraham, promising him the land of Canaan for an inheritance, and a son (Isaac) who would form a great nation. Isaac's son, Jacob, was blessed with twelve sons who fathered the twelve tribes of Israel.

Abraham is considered the father of the faith. It is interesting that, when the rich man in hell saw Abraham afar off, he addressed him as "Father Abraham" (Luke 16:24). Jews used this title because they recognized Abraham as the founder, or father, of their faith. This indicates that the rich man was likely a wealthy Jew whose earthly existence had focused on living the good life, all the while ignoring a poor, suffering beggar at the gate of his estate (Luke 16:20).

After Christ arose from the dead, He left no righteous souls in Abraham's bosom. Heroes of the faith, including the prophets and people in covenant with the God of Abraham who followed the laws of God penned by Moses, were released from this underworld location and transferred to paradise in the third heaven. The rich man, however, remained in his prison of torment.

In the kingdom of heaven, people will sit down with the prophets and patriarchs and hear astonishing inside information as they reveal stories that marked them as biblical legends. How did Noah build such a huge ark? How did Isaac feel when Abraham bound him on the altar? What did the opening of the Red Sea look like to Moses? What did Goliath look like to David as a teenager? Who were all the other men and women that Christ healed whose stories are not in the Bible? What happened in ages past, prior to Genesis 1:2?

Imagine the conversations you will have and the questions that will be answered. The mysteries that we now have no answers for finally will be revealed.

YOUR BEST YOU

The best news for many of us is that we will receive a new body at the resurrection. It will be the best one we'll ever have, and we get to keep it forever. We will look younger and will always remain youthful, healthy, and energetic. Excess fat is a physical manifestation that none of us appreciate. Good news! We won't find it on a resurrected body. No more dieting to keep off unwanted pounds. I say this in humor, but remember that even Paul said, "Lay aside the weight..." (Heb. 12:1).

In earlier days, there were no wrinkles on our faces and no crow's feet around our eyes. As we age, we look in a mirror and can't find that person we knew thirty years ago.

Like many of you, in my young days, I was athletic. I ran track, played football and basketball, and moved swiftly. Today I find myself walking a bit slower and being cautious that I don't trip on a rug or a step. My mother, at age eighty-two, fell on a wet floor in her house and broke her ankle and wrist. She had that strong, stubborn Italian nature, and after two surgeries and three months in a rehabilitation facility, she returned to work, assisted by a cane or a walker. In heaven, the fear of falling, injuring yourself, or developing a life-threatening illness will be a thing of the past. No fall will ever harm, no bruises will ever appear, and no disease will ever enter the resurrected body of a follower of Christ.

At death, the physical organs that remain in the body will decay and return to dust, just as God said the body of every person will do when they die (Gen. 3:19). When Christ returns to gather His living bride, His followers on the earth will know that the rapture is occurring when they experience "the shout, the voice of the archangel, and the trumpet of God" (1 Thess. 4:16).

Those who are already in paradise will be alerted moments before Christ returns for the living, as their spirits in paradise join with their resurrected bodies. The following verse explains: "For if we believe that

Jesus died and rose again, even so them also which sleep in Jesus will God bring with him" (1 Thessalonians 4:14 KJV).

Paul called resurrection from the dead a mystery. He used the analogy of a seed that must die in the ground before bringing forth a new plant. Through death, a body is laid to rest in the ground; but the spirit leaves the body until the day it enters a new, resurrected body. This is referred to as a *glorified* body—from a Greek word *doxazo*, referring to something with majesty and honor (1 Cor. 15:42-54). When we give honor to God, we glorify Him. When He gives us a new body, He is *honoring* us for faithfully serving Him (Rom. 8:17).

When we look in the mirror at an aging physical body, remember that we have something to look forward to. Your best body is yet to come, and this one you will keep in a world without end. Eternal life includes living forever in your new, imperishable body.

CHAPTER 6

UNLOCKING THE MYSTERY
OF INFANTS IN HEAVEN

The sudden and unexpected death of an infant or young child is the most difficult of all deaths, as it is something that we imagine should never occur. It creates an empty feeling for the parents who are now living on earth with part of their hearts in heaven.

When it comes to eternity, there is abundant evidence that the spirits of all infants and children go to heaven. Part of this thought stems from something biblical scholars call "the age of spiritual accountability." This is the age when an innocent child matures enough to become responsible for their beliefs and actions.

There has been debate for centuries about the age at which a child becomes accountable for their own sins and choices. I have heard various ages mentioned, such as five, ten, twelve, thirteen, or even older. Devout Jews recognize the significance of age twelve or thirteen. When a Jewish boy turns thirteen, the family celebrates with a bar mitzvah, meaning "son of commandment." A bat mitzvah, meaning "daughter of commandment," is for Jewish girls who turn twelve or thirteen. At this age, the child has all the rights and obligations of a Jewish adult. Before that age, the father of the child is responsible for the child's moral and spiritual instruction. Thirteen is also the age when most young people experience physical and emotional changes that we call puberty.

The Bible presents insight to assure us that children are special to the Lord and their spirits are brought to Him at death. One prime example is when David committed adultery with Bathsheba and she became pregnant with David's child, a son. Immediately after it was born, the infant was struck with sickness as judgment against David's sin. The newborn lived for seven days before passing. David had fasted for seven days for the child's healing, and when he died David said, "But now he is dead; why should I fast? Can I bring him back again? I shall go to him, but he will not return to me" (2 Samuel 12:23 - AMP)

David understood that when the child died, his tiny spirit was released from his body and carried in the arms of an angel to rest with the spirits of the righteous deceased in Abraham's bosom. David knew that he could not bring the infant back to life. But when he died, he would rejoin his son.

In the New Testament, Christ continually blessed the children. On one occasion, He revealed that children have their own personal angels:

"Take heed that you do not despise one of these little ones, for I say to you that in heaven their angels always see the face of My Father who is in heaven."

— MATTHEW 18:10 (NKJV)

The setting of this verse was the disciples asking Christ: Who is the greatest in the kingdom? Christ illustrated the answer by bringing a child before Him and speaking of their angels. This comforting truth indicates that angels are assigned to children, and their angels are continually before God's throne. Children are a major part of the kingdom of heaven:

"But Jesus said, "Let the little children come to Me, and do not forbid them; for of such is the kingdom of heaven." And He laid His hands on them and departed from there."

— MATTHEW 19:14-15 (NKJV)

If we apply this verse literally, it could mean that children can, and many will, receive Christ as their Savior at a young age. This is especially true for children who are raised in a strong Christian home. There is another possible application, though. In heaven are a countless number of children who were welcomed into the kingdom when they died. In 2020, around five million children under the age of five died, and many nations have a high infant mortality rate. The heavenly paradise for infants and children has a countless number of infants and children.

Adults who cannot receive Christ in the simple faith of a child will miss entering the kingdom of heaven. Jesus told us:

> *"Assuredly, I say to you, unless you are converted and become as little children, you will by no means enter the kingdom of heaven. Therefore, whoever humbles himself as this little child is the greatest in the kingdom of heaven. Whoever receives one little child like this in My name receives Me."*
>
> – MATTHEW 18:3-5 (NKJV)

Once again, we see Christ emphasizing the importance of children in the kingdom of heaven. There is also a firm and dangerous warning for anybody who would ever harm a child or hinder one from following Christ:

> *"Whoever receives one little child like this in My name receives Me. Whoever causes one of these little ones who believe in Me to sin, it would be better for him if a millstone were hung around his neck, and he were drowned in the depth of the sea."*
>
> – MATTHEW 18:5-6 (NKJV)

It would be well for drug dealers, traffickers, and child abusers to read this warning and take heed. Tying a millstone around a person's neck and throwing them into deep water was an extreme form of capital punishment among some groups in ancient times. Jesus was warning any abuser of children that they are in severe danger if they cause a child who believes in Jesus to sin.

CHILDREN IN HEAVEN

David knew that his infant child was with the Lord. God has assigned angels over children, and the kingdom of heaven is made up of children. I believe that all children who pass away are taken to the presence of the Lord and likely placed in a children's paradise.

An often-asked question is: Does the spirit of the deceased child remain a child in heaven, or does it mature to an adult?

Some evangelical theologians believe that when a child dies, the spirit will mature in heaven to a certain age (some suggest age twenty or thirty), and when we see them again, they will be young adults. However, this idea seems to contradict Jesus when He said that children are part of the kingdom of heaven, and the angels of children continually behold God's face (Matt. 18:10). Others believe there is a special paradise for the souls and spirits of infants and children, who will remain as children in the future kingdom.

In 1848, a woman named Marietta Davis lived in Berlin, New York. She became sick and fell into a coma, from which she did not awaken for nine days. When she awoke, she told of a journey she had taken to heaven. The account was published in a book titled, *Scenes Beyond the Grave*, edited by Gordon Lindsay.

In brief, Marietta had been carried to heaven by a guardian angel. There she saw numerous angels that were sent on errands of mercy. As she observed these angels on assignment, she was drawn to one angel who had ascended from earth to heaven, bearing in its arms a tiny infant spirit. The little spirit was being carried into a paradise of peace. She also saw an infant section of paradise, where every infant spirit has its own angel to care for it.

ARE THERE ANGELIC GUARDIANS?

Biblically, there are several types of angels that God has given different assignments. In Revelation 4:6-7, surrounding God's throne are four beasts called *living creatures*. They are full of eyes, and they have the faces of a man, a lion, an eagle, and an ox (calf). The word beasts here in Greek refers to a *living thing*. These are angelic beings that continually worship God before His throne.

There are also *cherubim*, which are angels assigned to guard divine things. These types of angels guarded the east entrance of the Garden of Eden (Gen. 3:24). Isaiah mentions *seraphim* as angels who proclaim the holiness of God (Isa. 6:1-3). A host of angels called *ministering spirits* are assigned to minister to those who are heirs of salvation (Heb. 1:13-14).

Some suggest that there are no guardian angels since they are not mentioned specifically in Scripture. However, there is ample scriptural *evidence* of guardian angels. In Daniel, the text speaks of *watchers* who observed activities in Babylon and eventually executed judgment on King Nebuchadnezzar (Dan. 4:17). The word watcher in Aramaic defines an angel who is alert, watching, guarding, and protecting.

Another example is an angel that God called "my angel" that was assigned to watch, protect, and keep the Israelites during their forty years in the wilderness (Exod. 23:20-23; 32:34). When Jacob was dying in Egypt, he prayed over his sons and mentioned "the angel which redeemed me from all evil" (Gen. 48:16). The angel that Jacob referred to was with him in all his journeys and visited him in visons and dreams (Gen. 28:12; 31:11; 32:1-2).

Angels ministered to Christ at the beginning of His ministry. At the end of His ministry, they supernaturally strengthened Him (Matt. 4:11 and Luke 22:42-43).

David spoke of specific angelic guardians when he penned: "The angel of the Lord encamps all around those who fear Him, and delivers them" (Psa. 34:7). The Hebrew word encamp means to *pitch a tent or to camp out*. This passage indicates there are angels that remain camped out at certain locations for specific assignments.

Christ was speaking of children when He said that in heaven "their angels" continually see the face of God. If children's angels are commissioned to watch and protect them on earth, then how can they continually see the face of the Heavenly Father?

One implication of that statement could be that the children are deceased, and their spirits are now with the Lord. In that case, the angel assigned to that child would be in heaven, and therefore would continually see the face of God. When a child passes from this life, a guardian angel carries the spirit of the child to heaven, because angels are involved in transporting spirits of the righteous when they die. When the beggar died at the rich man's gate, angels carried his spirit to his resting place in Abraham's bosom (Luke 16:22).

When Moses died in the plains of Pisgah in Jordan, according to Jude 9, there was a strong dispute in the spirit world concerning his body. At death, the spirit of Moses departed, but his body remained on the ground. The archangel Michael engaged in a sharp contention with Satan over the body of Moses, as Michael prevented Satan from seizing the body of Israel's 120-year-old leader and prophet. God himself buried Moses in an unknown location (Deut. 34:6). If the people had discovered Moses' dead body, they might have built a monument in Jordan and either delayed entering the Promised Land or remained in Moab and Edom, falling short of their land inheritance.

AMAZING STORIES OF CHILDREN DEPARTING

When I was a young traveling evangelist, I met many interesting people with incredible faith building stories. One such story was of a family who had a beautiful young girl who was unable to walk due to serious birth defects. At age five, she became ill and was taken to a hospital where the family was brought to see her for the last time. Soon she was declared dead. The family cleared the room to allow medical personnel to prepare her body, but the family's pastor asked if he could remain for just a few minutes. He was given a short amount of time to be in the room.

The pastor was frightened when he saw a shadowy figure shrouded in black step through the wall. He thought, "What is this? This cannot be from God, and it cannot touch the spirit of this child!" Suddenly he saw two long shafts of light descend from the ceiling into the hospital room. Instantly the dark figure vanished. The two light beams formed into beautiful angels, one on each side of the child's bed.

These angels placed their bright wings under the hospital bed and lifted their wings upward. The bed was no hindrance for them to pass though. Their wings of light went through the body of the child, releasing her spirit from her body. She was resting on the wings of two angels as they lifted her spirit and carried it on their wings. Her spirit was perfect and had no deformities. She looked at the pastor and smiled as she was carried up to the ceiling where all three—two angels and the little girl—vanished.

NINE-YEAR-OLD CHARLES

Years ago, on our Manna-fest telecast, Theo Carter, a great man of God and minister of the Gospel, relayed this remarkable story. In the 1940s, Theo's nine-year-old son, Charles Edward, was shooting fireworks in the road when a truck driver accidently ran over the little fellow and killed him. Theo and his wife Thelma were strong believers, but they greatly grieved the loss of their precious son.

Decades later Thelma was sent to a hospital in Louisville, Kentucky for heart surgery. While she was on the operating table, she died. After making several attempts to revive her, the doctors pronounced her dead and covered her with a sheet as they prepared her body to be taken to the morgue.

Then, to the shock of the doctors, she came back to life. Medical professionals later determined that she had been dead approximately twenty-one minutes. During this time, her spirit had been to heaven, and she returned with a marvelous experience to tell.

While there, she saw her son Charles Edward, who looked exactly the way he did when he died forty-three years earlier. He saw her and greeted her as "Mom." Charles was with other deceased believers whom Thelma and Theo had known during their lifetime. Charles informed his mother that he and other children play on the streets of gold.

Thelma noticed that a minister, who had been a good friend of the family before he died, was standing with her son. Charles told her, "Mom, he is my guardian up here. He helps watch over me." To Theo, this was a revelation that loved ones and friends who have passed away are able to interact with and help care for children who are now in paradise. The experience also showed him that it is possible for children in heaven to remain the same age as they were when they died on earth.

Theo Carter, the father of this child and the husband of Thelma, was a man of impeccable integrity and holy living, and he told this story throughout the holiness churches in Eastern Kentucky.

WILL CHILDREN GET OLDER EVENTUALLY?

Will all small children remain small children throughout eternity, or can they eventually mature into an adult? Assuming a person can select the age that they want to appear when they arrive in heaven, any older person would likely choose to be younger. But a child has never been an adult, so they might choose to remain the age they were when they left the earth.

As for a very young child, let's say age five and under, consider that the parents who lose a child at such a young age never were able to spend time with the child and enjoy the experience of watching them grow up. I do believe that God will give you an opportunity to spend time with them while they are a child, so that you can enjoy what you missed on earth. Perhaps, after a period of time, the child might grow to be an adult, just as they would have done on earth had they lived to be older. We cannot be certain because some of this remains a mystery.

When David noted that he would one day go to be with his deceased infant son, he never revealed what age his son would appear when he saw him again. However, remember that Jesus does speak of children in the kingdom.

Once we arrive in heaven after our earthly departure, we will enjoy a wonderful reunion with family and friends who are awaiting our arrival. We can be assured that the reunion will include all the infants and children who made the celestial journey ahead of us.

CHAPTER 7

THE SPIRIT OF A MISCARRIED OR ABORTED CHILD

Medically, a miscarriage is defined as the spontaneous loss of a baby before the twentieth week of pregnancy. The Mayo Clinic says that ten to twenty percent of known pregnancies end in miscarriage, and many occur very early in pregnancy.

One of the common questions people have asked over the years concerns miscarriages. People want to know if the fetus has an eternal spirit, and if so, will they see their infant in heaven. Some suggest this question cannot be answered, but I disagree.

Humans have a body, soul, and spirit. The body is the physical shell that holds the soul and spirit, as well as the organs and blood. The life of the flesh is in the blood (Lev. 17:11). The soul is the element that gives us our emotions, and it is where our thoughts and actions originate—in our mind. We are told to renew this part of our being daily (Romans 12:2). The spirit is the breath of God that abides within the body and enables a person to desire, connect with, and know God. The spirit is evidence that the fetus—the child growing in the womb—is not just flesh, blood, and tissue, but an eternal creation.

There are at least three opinions about when the soul and spirit enter the infant's body: at conception; six months after conception; or when the umbilical cord is cut. Shockingly, there are some who claim that the spirit does not enter a child until one year of age.

TERMS AND WORDS

The common medical term for an unborn baby growing in the mother's womb is *fetus*. One of the Latin and Greek words for fetus means *unborn offspring*.

Those who promote abortion view the unborn as something not fully human that can be extracted from the womb and discarded if the mother so chooses. The common pro-abortion demand today is to accept full term abortions, with some suggesting the parent should have the choice to legally exterminate ("abort") the child after birth, even up to one year of age.

As Christians, we must not be swayed by the secular worldview of life, whether in or out of the womb. It is our obligation to search Scripture for our foundation of truth. Clearly, in the eyes of God, those who are still in the womb are living human beings and not just a clump of soulless cells.

In Genesis 25:21-22, Isaac's wife Rebekah was pregnant with twins. As the two boys were growing inside her womb, they "struggled together within her" (Gen 25:22). Notice that the inspired Word of God refers to the two sons as children, even while they were yet unborn. The Hebrew word is *ben*, the common Hebrew word for son (it also means offspring). It is the same word used when listing the names of the sons of a father throughout Scripture (Gen. 10:21-23).

In Luke 1:43, Elizabeth was addressing Mary, who had just been visited by an angel who informed her that she would be supernaturally impregnated with holy seed to carry the future Messiah. Elizabeth called Mary "the mother of my Lord" *nine months* before Jesus was born in Bethlehem. Mary was called "a mother" as soon as she conceived, and not just when she physically birthed the infant.

Elizabeth and her husband Zacharias, both advanced in years, prayed for many years to conceive a child. The Lord blessed Elizabeth to conceive, giving her and Zacharias a son named John. Elizabeth was six months pregnant with John when Mary visited her and announced her own pregnancy. In Luke 1:41-44, Elizabeth felt John physically move in her womb and said to Mary, "The babe leaped in my womb for joy."

The Greek word for babe in that verse is *brephos.* Luke uses the word four times when referring to both John the Baptist and Christ. The same Greek word is used by Luke, who was a medical doctor, to identify the infant developing *in* the womb, as well as the infant after he or she has been born and is *outside* the womb (Luke 2:12, 16). The word *brephos* refers to an unborn child, a newborn child, and an infant that is a little older (Luke 1:41, 2:12, and 18:15; Acts 7:19; 2 Tim. 3:15). This is not a word thrown around lightly. It describes a living child, whether in or out of the womb.

The truth is that the Bible calls a child *a living human,* whether it is *in* the womb or *outside* the womb. Only a living human can leap in the womb for joy. The angel Gabriel had informed John's father, Zacharias, that John would be "filled with the Holy Ghost, even from his mother's womb" (Luke 1:15). The Holy Spirit fills a person by imparting power into the human spirit and abiding in them. To be filled from his mother's womb would require that John have an eternal spirit already residing within his small body while he was growing within his mother. The infilling of John occurred when he was six months of age, yet still in his mother's womb. At the same time, Elizabeth was also filled with the Holy Spirit (Luke 1:41). Notice that the same thing that happened to the mother spiritually also impacted the child growing within her.

CONCEPTION AND BIRTH ARE BOTH MARKED

We all know that biological conception occurs when the seed of the male joins with the egg of the female and results in fertilization, and thus the formation of a new and living person. In Scripture, the moment of conception is marked as the beginning of life. Without the life force from the Creator, there is no moment of conception and no pregnancy.

Genesis 25:21-22, 2 Kings 19:3, and Ruth 1:11 speak of children in the womb. Job 3:3 speaks of the time when a male child (Job) was conceived. The infant was considered a son at conception and a son after his birth. Throughout Scripture, the infant is a living human being, both inside and outside the womb.

God alone has the attribute of foreknowledge, meaning that He has detailed information on every person before they are conceived. He knows their gender, and He knows their name. Here are biblical examples:

- Before their son was conceived, Abraham and Sarah were told that Sarah would bear a son and his name would be called Isaac (Gen. 17:19).

- Before Samson's birth, his mother and father were informed they would have a son and he would be a Nazarite (Judges 13).

- Before John was conceived, the angel Gabriel informed his father that their child would be a son named John, who would come in the spirit of Elijah and be filled with the Spirit from his mother's womb (Luke 1:13).

- The angel Gabriel brought Mary a message that she would conceive a son whose name would be Jesus, and He would save His people from their sins (Matt. 1:21).

Note that in three of the four examples—Isaac, John, and Jesus—the names of the sons were revealed before conception. This demonstrates the foreknowledge of God in a child's conception, birth, and destiny.

In two Old Testament prophecies, the Holy Spirit revealed the names of two important future leaders, hundreds of years before their birth. One was a coming king of Judah named Josiah (1 Kings 13:2). Another was named Cyrus, a Persian king who would have a prophetic destiny (Isaiah 44:28). In Jeremiah 1:5, God told Jeremiah, "Before I formed you in the womb I knew you; before you were born I sanctified you; I ordained you a prophet to the nations."

THE SPIRIT WITHIN INFANTS

In Ecclesiastes 11:5, Solomon wrote: "As thou knowest not what is the way of the spirit, nor how the bones do grow in the womb of her that is with child: even so thou knowest not the works of God who maketh all."

The spirit and the bones grow in the womb. Look at the miracle of the incarnation. Jesus, who pre-existed with God, left His position in heaven to enter the womb of a young virgin. For nine months His body grew within Mary until the time that He would be born and revealed in Bethlehem. Paul wrote about Christ: "A body thou hast prepared me" (Heb. 10:5). The body was prepared within Mary and revealed to the world at birth.

Paul penned an interesting observation when he said, "For I was alive without the law once: but when the commandment came, sin revived, and I died" (Romans 7:9).

The time that Paul was "alive without the law" was when he was a child, innocent and with no conscience or conviction of sin. We would call this before the age of accountability. I believe this age varies, as each child has a different level of maturity and comprehension.

Moving from childhood into maturity, Paul reached an age where he understood the law and the consequences of breaking the law. The conscience is the inner voice that convicts or rebukes a person when they know they are sinning or breaking the law. Children, whose minds are simple and whose hearts are sincere, are innocent until they mature to perceive and understand, not just parental rights and wrongs, but the laws of God and man.

Christ understood this when He ministered and when parents brought their children to be blessed by Him. He said that the kingdom of heaven is made up of children (Matt. 19:14). Christ informed His disciples, "Unless you are converted and become as little children, you will by no means enter the kingdom of heaven" (Matt. 18:3).

It is clear in the examples throughout both the Old and New Testament that the soul and spirit enter the womb the moment of conception. The body is simply the shell that one day will return to the dust of the ground. The soul and spirit are eternal, sent from God, and necessary for the body to have life.

WHAT ABOUT A MISCARRIAGE?

While Scripture does not use the word miscarriage, the King James Version does speak of an *untimely birth* in Job 3:16. This word is rendered *stillborn* or *miscarriage*. When Job lost his wealth, his ten children, and his health, he began to curse the day he was born (Job 3:1). He said, "Or why was I not hidden like a stillborn child, like infants who never saw light? There the wicked cease from troubling, and there the weary are at rest. There the prisoners rest together; they do not hear the voice of the oppressor. The small and great are there, and the servant is free from his master" (Job 3:16-19).

Job knew that an infant who dies will see no wickedness and be at rest. The rest that he speaks of refers to the soul and spirit remaining in a compartment (in Job's day, the place was Abraham's bosom) where the person ceases from their labor. The word "prisoners" means the captives—the souls and spirits of the deceased. These are the souls that Christ ministered to during His three days and nights in the heart of the earth. Notice that both the small and great are there. The word *small* in Hebrew is *qaton*, and it means the least, the little, young, or youngest. This is the place where David's infant son went when he died seven days after his birth.

In another verse, Job 3:11 speaks of an unborn infant dying: "Why died I not from the womb? Why did I not give up the ghost when I came out of the belly?"

Job poses the same question to the Almighty in Job 10:18, as he regrets that he didn't die before he was born: "Wherefore then hast thou brought me forth out of the womb? Oh that I had given up the ghost, and no eye had seen me!"

This is another biblical indicator that, both in and out of the womb, the infant has a spirit that, when taken from the body, results in physical death. The eternal spirit dwells within the infant's small body while it is in the mother's womb.

OUR PERSONAL EXPERIENCE

Pam and I were married for eight years before she became pregnant with our first child, our son Jonathan. In the late 1980s before he was conceived, I had two separate dreams in which I saw two little girls. One appeared to be about five years old and the other looked younger. One child seemed strong and in charge, while the other looked weak and appeared to have some type of bodily defect. I asked the healthy-looking girl, "What's your name?" and she replied, "I'm Amanda—the little girl you're going to have." I asked about the other girl and she replied, "This is my sister, Rochelle."

I told Pam about the dream and suggested that it appears we will have two girls in the future. We had a book of baby names, so we looked up Amanda and Rochelle. We discovered that Rochelle means "little rock," or "from a little stone." We started preparing for a girl.

Instead, we were blessed with a son.

Eleven years passed, and due to my intense travel schedule, we had not considered having more children. After returning from a lengthy trip, I was lying down in the master bedroom, when suddenly I felt the hand of a small child on my left ankle. It seemed to be trying to balance itself, yet no child was present. I sat up and told Pam what happened. I said, "I believe this is a sign we are supposed to have another child."

At age thirty-eight Pam became pregnant. We informed our family, friends, and ministry partners who knew about the dream from eleven years earlier, and they were in agreement that the girl was coming. We thought we could possibly have twins, although the two girls in the dream appeared to be different ages.

Several weeks into the pregnancy, on a Monday in November, we were in Pigeon Forge, Tennessee setting up for our biggest meeting of the year. That was the day Pam had a miscarriage.

After this sad event, Pam felt that, both emotionally and physically, she would not be able to carry another child. However, she did become pregnant again. In the seventh month her doctor placed her on bed rest. I told Pam this would be a girl, and since I saw a healthy girl in my earlier dream, she should not be fearful. On August 2, 2001, our healthy daughter arrived and we named her Amanda, based on the dream from over a decade earlier.

We will not be having other children, so the question for us was, what happened to Rochelle? Were we supposed to have another child, or was Rochelle the child who was miscarried? Several circumstances seemed to indicate Rochelle was that child. When Pam asked the Lord why the infant was taken and never given a chance to live on earth, she was reminded of the dreams in which Amanda was strong, but Rochelle looked weak and sickly.

THE BABY GIRL IN HEAVEN

Many years later we received a touching letter from a woman named Leisia from Oak Hills, California who did not know about Pam's miscarriage. The letter moved me to tears, while at the same time it gave me great joy.

Leisia's only son named Levi passed away, bringing her a season of terrible grief. She had prayed and prayed for the Lord to allow her to see Levi in heaven. One day she had an "out of the body experience" (see 2 Cor. 12:1-4) and was taken to heaven where she saw her sister-in-law who had passed away seven months before her son. Leisia asked her if she knew where Levi was, and the sister-in-law replied that she did. Leisia described being in one location in heaven, then suddenly being in another location.

She came to her son who was sitting in a large chair. He ran to her and they hugged. She said that in heaven, you don't have to talk, as you can read the other person's thoughts and feelings. Oddly, Levi was growing a beard. This was amazing to her, as the medicine he had taken on earth caused him to be unable to grow facial hair. She then wrote the following:

> "This is not the reason for my letter today. The Lord moved on my heart to write to you after another heavenly experience I had yesterday. I was praying before daybreak, in the early hours of Friday, September 20, 2013. While I was praying, I either slipped off into a dream or I had a vision, and I found myself in the waiting room of a grand assembly of God's people in heaven. I sat down next to a beautiful little girl. She had a light complexion, beautiful eyes, a dainty nose, and the loveliest thick black curly hair. But she also had the wisdom of the ancients. When I sat next to her, I knew that she was Perry and Pam Stone's daughter. Nevertheless, she was not Amanda.

She smiled very big, and as I sat down next to her, she said, 'I know who you are. You are a godly woman....'

"The only thing I know is that somehow you both have a gorgeous little girl in heaven who is waiting for you...."

In my dream many years ago, Rochelle had dark hair. However, I also recalled that she looked weak in her eyes and not as strong as Amanda. In my mind I still can remember what she looked like. In the dream Rochelle was holding a small stuff animal.

The story reached another astonishing level in 2014 in Griffin, Georgia. I met a doctor who is a wonderful artist, and she brought a selection of artwork for me to look at. When I saw one that she had drawn of a little girl holding a small stuffed animal, I almost went into shock. The drawing looked nearly identical to Rochelle as I had seen her in my dream years ago. I now own that drawing. I still cry occasionally when I look at it.

MISCARRIAGE – ANOTHER CHILD IN HEAVEN

Bart Green is a book and screenplay writer whose grandfather was a noted minister named G.W. Lane, who passed away many years ago. G.W. never wore a three-piece suit, but he was buried in one. Years after his grandfather's death, Bart began to suffer some medical problems and, on one occasion while in the hospital, he felt that he died and his spirit briefly left his body.

During this "out of the body" experience, Bart found himself in a thick fog walking toward a bright light. He came upon the silhouette of two men talking to one another. As the fog lifted, he saw that one of the men was his grandfather, G.W. Lane, and he was wearing a three-piece suit. G.W. told Bart that God was not finished with his work on earth, and he revealed things that Bart would complete. At the time these were things he was not working on, but later began to manifest.

G.W. began to walk away out of the fog and into the light. Barton attempted to follow him, but G.W. turned and told Barton, "No, you cannot go with us." G.W. did say one more thing that stunned Barton. He said, "I should tell you. Your son is proud of you."

Barton sat across from my desk at the Voice of Evangelism office and told me this story. He said, "At first the part about the son threw me off. This was a very real experience, but I never had a son. Then I remembered that, when I was married, my wife had a miscarriage. It is apparent that the child was a boy and today he is in heaven."

To me, the most surprising part of this story is that his son was aware of who his father is and the things he is doing on earth. How this is possible remains a mystery.

WHAT ABOUT ABORTIONS?

Since the 1973 Supreme Court ruling on Roe versus Wade that legalized abortion on demand, and then the overturning of the decision in 2022, the United States population has remained divided on this issue. Most of the people who promote abortion say that it should be legal at any time and for any reason, and they treat it as though abortion is a minor medical procedure. Those with biblical knowledge and a kingdom mentality view abortion as wrong and believe that every life, in any stage of life, is important.

We have been given a unique honor above all other of God's creation. We alone are made in the image and the likeness of God (Gen. 1:26). We have a characteristic that separates us from the angels, and that is the ability to procreate and bring to life another human who has within it an eternal soul and spirit.

Psalm 127:3 says, "Children are a heritage of the Lord." From Proverbs 17:6 we read, "Children's children are the crown of old men; and the glory of children are their fathers."

Children are a gift, a joy, and an honor. Yet, millions have aborted their own offspring, made in their own likeness and the image of God, and have destroyed their own future in the process. The psalmist wrote a fantastic word about his own conception and development in his mother's womb:

> *"For you formed my inward parts; you covered me in my mother's womb. I will praise you, for I am fearfully and wonderfully made; marvelous are your works, and that my soul knows very well. My frame was not hidden from you, when I was made in secret, and skillfully wrought in the lowest parts of the earth. Your eyes saw my substance, being yet unformed. And in your book they were all written, the days fashioned for me, when as yet there were none of them."*
>
> — PSALMS 139:13-16

CHILDREN ARE A SEED

Throughout Scripture, God identified a future child as the seed before the baby was conceived in the womb. Abraham and his sons were circumcised in the flesh of their foreskins, and all Hebrew infant sons were required to be circumcised on the eighth day after their birth as a sign of their covenant with God (Gen. 17:1-12).

When a Hebrew son grew into a man, married, and consummated with his wife, his seed (sperm) would pass through the "sign" of the covenant (the mark of circumcision on his flesh) when his seed entered his wife. Thus, the seed that would eventually form a child through conception was *marked* for blessing by the Lord *before* the infant was ever conceived.

This same spiritual principle is found in Genesis 14, in the narrative where Abraham paid tithes in Salem (Jerusalem) to Melchizedek.

Hebrews 7:8-9 reveals that Abraham paid tithes for Levi, who was still in his father's loins when Abraham met Melchizedek. At that time, Isaac, Jacob, and his son Levi had not been born, as Levi would be the third generation from Abraham. This verse indicates that the actions of a father impact future generations. This is the reason God warned Israel that He would visit the iniquities of the father on the third and fourth generations of those who hate Him (Exod. 20:5).

In society's so-called progressive way of thinking, a lie has emerged that the spirit of an infant enters the body once the umbilical cord is cut and the infant breathes its first breath outside the womb. This idea is promoted because it gives a reason to justify abortion up to nine months. Of course, this idea is not found anywhere in Scripture.

As previously noted throughout Scripture, the Bible marks the moment of *conception* as the beginning of life, and not just the moment the birth process takes place nine months later. The King James translation of the Bible speaks many times of a son or a child being conceived. The word conceive in the New Testament commonly refers to procreating, and it alludes to the moment that the seed and the egg began the process of creating a new and living person.

God foreknows the child and sometimes revealed in Scripture that He had a name or a destiny chosen before the child was born, or while the infant was still in the womb. This was evident with Jeremiah when God said, "Before I formed you in the womb I knew you; before you were born I sanctified you; I ordained you a prophet to the nations" (Jeremiah 1:5 NKJV).

The psalmist wrote: "For you formed my inward parts; you covered me in my mother's womb. I will praise you, for I am fearfully and wonderfully made" (Psalms 139:13-14 NKJV). The word *covered* (some translations say *knit together*) alludes to *weaving together*. It is a reference to a person sowing pieces of cloth together to form a beautiful garment.

When we view a sonogram of an infant in the womb, we observe how the child moves and grows and how its body is formed. To go from a seed to bringing forth a child with a living soul and eternal spirit is a process which is nothing short of a miracle.

Countless husbands and wives have wanted to conceive a child but have been unable for various reasons. The nation of Israel was born from the wombs of women who once were barren:

- Sarah was barren, and she conceived and bore Isaac at age ninety.

- Rebekah was barren and conceived twin sons—Jacob and Esau.

- Rachel was barren and conceived two sons—Joseph and Benjamin.

- Hannah was barren and gave birth to Samuel and six other children.

- Elizabeth was barren and gave birth to John the Baptist.

In certain instances, the women who were barren cried out to God for a child, and the Lord "opened the womb."

The greatest conception miracle was that of Jesus Christ, whose mother was a virgin. The seed placed in Mary by the Holy Spirit was the seed of the Word of God. John wrote: "The Word became flesh and dwelt among us" (John 1:14). When the Holy Spirit overshadowed Mary, God was breathing into her body the seed of Christ. Conception occurs when God breaths the breath of life on the seed and the egg. The fact that the fetus is growing proves that the child is vibrant and alive.

When Gabriel told Mary that she would have a son, he said, "That Holy One who is to be born will be called the Son of God" (Luke 1:35).

The King James translation says, "that holy thing." There are numerous biblical definitions of the word "thing." But this word is *hagios* in Greek, which is the word for "holy, sacred, consecrated, and blameless." The angel was not calling Jesus a thing, as some lifeless object growing in Mary, but was identifying the holiness of the person she was going to carry.

THE SIX MONTHS THEORY

Some people theorize that the soul and spirit are placed within the infant at about six months, when the child has developed certain abilities. They base this idea on statements made by Elizabeth concerning John the Baptist. As mentioned previously, Elizabeth was six months pregnant with John when the baby leaped for joy in Elizabeth's womb (Luke 1:15). The Bible says that John was "filled with the Holy Ghost from his mother's womb."

According to New Testament verses that refer to the infilling of the Holy Spirit, He comes into your human spirit (fills you with His presence) to abide. The New Testament speaks of a prayer language, or praying in unknown tongues. Paul wrote of his own experience, saying that when he prays in an unknown tongue, his spirit is praying (1 Cor.14:14). As *a spirit*, the Holy Spirit enters the temple of the human body to dwell within the human spirit.

Baby John obviously had a soul and spirit at six months, or he could not have been "filled from his mother's womb." If John had been only a mass of tissue that became a person at some point in the future, then he could not have been filled with the Spirit. When John leaped, his spirit was already in his body as it grew in his mother's womb.

A third belief of some who accept late term abortion is that the soul and spirit are not in the infant until after the umbilical cord is severed and the infant breaths on its own outside the womb. Their theory that the eternal spirit enters the child after birth gives them the perceived "freedom" to abort a child, right up until the time of birth, since they consider the infant a non-eternal being, as long as it is not outside the womb and breathing on its own.

Years ago, a member of Planned Parenthood resigned after watching an abortion on ultrasound. In the late 1970s, a well-known doctor named Bernard Nathanson stopped performing abortions after using ultrasound during an abortion. He became a pro-life activist who called abortion "the most atrocious holocaust in the history of the United States."

Nathanson observed on the ultrasound that the infant attempted to protect itself from the intrusion of the outside force. Based on this, he directed and narrated a film titled *The Silent Scream*.

On ultrasound, little ones are seen moving, kicking, sucking their thumb, and performing other typical infant activities in the womb. The life force of the soul and spirit are absolutely inside the infant, or else it would show no signs of life within the womb.

Under the Law of Moses, there were penalties for harming the unborn in the mother's womb:

> *"If men strive, and hurt a woman with child, so that her fruit depart from her, and yet no mischief follow: he shall be surely punished, according as the woman's husband will lay upon him; and he shall pay as the judges determine. And if any mischief follow, then thou shalt give life for life, eye for eye, tooth for tooth, hand for hand, foot for foot, burning for burning, wound for wound, stripe for stripe."*
>
> — Exodus 21:22-25

The spirit comes from God and returns to God. Solomon wrote of death, "Then shall the dust return to the earth as it was: and the spirit shall return unto God who gave it" (Eccl. 12:7). Since the eternal spirit enters the womb of the mother and breathes life at conception, then if anything occurs within the womb to take the life of the child, the spirit of the child goes back to God. The spirit does not become a vapor, a floating light, or a cherub with a harp. This is the spirit of an actual human being.

We are all unique; no two fingerprints are alike. No footprints are alike. The same is true with the design of our eyes, and even the shape of our teeth. Each person is created so that there is nobody else exactly like us.

Stories abound of people who had a near death experience and saw a child or other family member who never survived to live on earth, but the child is presently in heaven with other children their age. They are doing what children do—exactly what children would be doing on earth.

If you have ever lost a child of any age through death, you will always feel that part of your heart is missing. When you arrive in heaven and see the child again, you will reunite with the missing part of your life and be made complete again.

CHAPTER 8

MEMORIES RETAINED AND MEMORIES LOST

There is a chasm of difference between the deaths of a *righteous* person and an *unrighteous* person. I have attended funerals (home-goings is the term I prefer) of godly, righteous believers who departed this life. People are sad for the loss, but also filled with faith and anticipation, knowing where the believer is going and that we have the opportunity to see them again.

At my dad's home going, the atmosphere at the T.L. Lowery Foundation Center was one of sadness for the family, as we were already missing his jovial smile and raspy voice that could pierce heaven with prayer. Yet, joy prevailed over our sorrow, knowing that the loved ones remaining who follow Christ will one day rejoin him in the eternal City of God. This is the promise for a believer.

The funeral of a known sinner or rejecter of the Gospel, however, has a completely different feel, as a somber chill permeates the atmosphere. Sometimes an uncomfortable silence numbs the air. Good things might be said about the departed person—he was a good father...he worked hard...people in the community liked him.... But it is impossible for those who are biblically knowledgeable to rejoice, knowing that the personal life of the departed was contrary to every biblical commandment, and the person likely left this life without a redemptive covenant.

Here is what the Bible says about a redeemed soul who is transported from *earthly life to eternal life*: "Precious in the sight of the Lord is the death of His saints" (Psalm 116:15). Solomon wrote, "The memory of the righteous is blessed, but the name of the wicked will rot." (Prov. 10:7).

There is much said in Scripture about the departure of the unrighteous:

"His remembrance shall perish from the earth, and he shall have no name in the street."

— Job 18:17

"The face of the LORD is against them that do evil, to cut off the remembrance of them from the earth."

— Psalms 34:16

"Cast away from you all the transgressions which you have committed, and get yourselves a new heart and a new spirit. For why should you die, O house of Israel? For I have no pleasure in the death of one who dies," says the Lord God. "Therefore turn and live!"

— Ezekiel 18:31-32

Long after a godly person has departed, pleasant memories of the individual are still recalled on earth. The righteous are missed by their families, who anticipate seeing them again. The unrighteous, however, leave no fragrance of pleasant memories when their existence on earth ceases.

Consider the following people. What is the first thought that comes to mind when you hear their names?

Adolph Hitler. After nearly eighty years, he is still recalled as a demonic tyrant responsible for the destruction of countries and the deaths of millions of people during his reign of terror.

Joseph Stalin. This Soviet Marxist dictator is infamous after seventy years because he was a brutal dictator, also responsible for the deaths of tens of millions of people.

Roman Emperor Nero. Those familiar with church history have read about the violent escapades of this psychopathic emperor. He died in AD 68, but after all this time, people still speak of him as a wicked man.

Judas Iscariot. His name is connected to one word: betrayal. Almost 2,000 years after he hung himself, Judas' legacy is that of a thief and a betrayer of Christ.

Historical memories associated with those long-dead, wicked men are Holocaust, Marxism-Communism, the beheading of Paul and persecution of the saints, and treachery for thirty pieces of silver. There are no pleasant thoughts, kind words, or special anniversaries celebrated in their honor. Their names are dishonored, their memories are cursed, and there are no memorials commemorating their kindness to humanity.

If, in your own bloodline, you have a deceased relative who was violent, abusive, unforgiving, and continually angry, something within the hearts of the surviving relatives wants those negative and troubling memories to fade. Families want to move forward and fulfill their remaining days on earth in peace, without having a reminder of the torment that person put them through.

There is a good reason for this mental separation. First, an emotionally or physically wounded person needs to heal, which is difficult if the abuse and hatred are replayed over and over in the person's mind. These terrible memories can plant seeds of despondency that birth the fruit of depression or mental and spiritual bondage. The victims need to be healed of the trauma that person caused.

Also, for those living in a redemptive covenant of eternal life through Christ, the thought of any loved one being separated from God eternally is a heavy weight for the mind to bear. Only the Holy

Spirit can bring comfort in such instances and cause a believer to move forward with their own assignments.

MEMORY IN HEAVEN

People often wonder if they will know their loved ones in heaven, or if they will be aware that a family member died lost. The narrative of the transfiguration of Christ may hold a clue.

Christ invited Peter, James, and John to join Him on a mountain for a secret meeting with two of Israel's most celebrated prophets: Moses and Elijah. The day grew long and the journey up the mountain stretched the physical strength of the three disciples. They fell asleep after reaching the top. When they awoke, Elijah and Moses were standing with Christ, speaking to Him about His future death in Jerusalem. Elijah had been transported alive in a whirlwind and a chariot of fire about seven hundred years earlier (2 Kings 2). Moses had died 1,500 years prior, and his body was secretly buried by God Himself in the valley below Mount Nebo, in what is today the country of Jordan (Deut. 34:5-7).

Thus, Elijah was brought out of the third heaven for this encounter, and Moses' spirit was brought up from Abraham's bosom, an underground subterranean world where the departed souls of the righteous once rested prior to the resurrection of Christ (Luke 16:19-31). Moses was brought up from the underworld of sheol, and Elijah was brought down from the upper region of heaven.

When Peter awoke, he immediately identified both Moses and Elijah without anyone telling him who they were. There were no paintings, etchings, photographs, or other known images of these two prophets; thus, Peter's ability to recognize them was *spiritual discernment* from the Holy Spirit that quickened his understanding of the men's identities (Luke 9:28-36).

This may explain how believers will recognize one another in heaven, even the saints of old, without being formally introduced. We are told that God knows the names and number of all the stars (Psalms 147:4), and He has numbered the hairs of your head (Matt. 10:30). Eternal knowledge far surpasses human intellect, so outside of human limitations, the human spirit will advance in understanding, once we become "the spirits of the just (righteous) made perfect" (Heb. 12:23).

One New Testament verse written by the Apostle Paul answers the question of whether we will know one another in heaven. In 1 Corinthians 13, Paul explains that spiritual gifts designed to edify the church are temporary and only useful until the return of Christ (1 Cor. 13:10). He emphasized the eternal characteristic of love that will abide forever. He then revealed how we will be known when that which is perfect (Christ and His kingdom) comes:

"For now we see in a mirror, dimly, but then face to face. Now I know in part, but then I shall know just as I also am known."

— 1 CORINTHIANS 13:12

Presently, our knowledge is *in part*, another way of saying that we have *partial knowledge*. When we are face to face with Christ, the one who is perfect, then partial understanding will be done away with, and we will have complete knowledge. All questions of "why" will be answered, such as, Why was my family member not healed? Why did my child pass away early and not live out his life? Why did I suffer so much? Why were some of my prayers not answered?

Paul points out that he will be known as he is known. That word *known* is *epiginosko* in Greek, and it means "to fully know, to recognize, to become fully acquainted with, to acknowledge." This ability in eternity to recognize people whom you know, as well as those you have never met, is part of the activity of the Holy Spirit. We read:

"The Spirit Himself bears witness with our spirit that we are children of God."

— ROMANS 8:16

Bears witness with means that our spirit testifies in support of the fact. A *witness* is used in a court setting when the person has evidence that can either justify or condemn the one being prosecuted. It is the Holy Spirit Himself that correctly identifies true believers in any gathering of people. No doubt you have experienced being somewhere, perhaps a mall or a restaurant, where you have encountered a person you've never met before, yet you know in your spirit that person is a believer. It has nothing to do with their outward appearance or any activity they are engaged in, but the Holy Spirit, like a magnet, draws believers toward each other and causes them to recognize Christ in the other person.

There are nine gifts of the Holy Spirit referred to in 1 Corinthians 12:7-10. These nine gifts can be divided into three categories: mind gifts, power gifts, and vocal gifts. The mind gifts, for example, are word of wisdom, word of knowledge, and discerning of spirits. When my father was living, I saw these three gifts operate during his pulpit ministry. The Holy Spirit would reveal minute details concerning a person's family or situation. These were revelations that Dad had no personal knowledge of, but God knew. Through my dad, the Holy Spirit released a word of knowledge or discernment about the types of spirits attacking the individual.

Jesus operated in these gifts when, *by the Spirit,* He saw Nathanial sitting under a fig tree when Jesus was not physically present to actually see him there (see John 1:44-50). Christ discerned the root cause of a sickness when He prayed for a woman who was bent over for eighteen years. She had never been prayed for by her rabbi or released from her physical weakness until Christ identified the culprit as a *spirit of infirmity* (Luke 13:11-12).

The human spirit is the spiritual antenna that connects the earthly with the heavenly, and the Holy Spirit sparks the flame of knowledge in the mind of a believer. Presently, we see through a dull mirror because we have limited knowledge and understanding. But once the human spirit is outside the limitations of the body (through death or the catching away of the believer - 1 Thess. 4:16-17), our knowledge vault will be unlocked, and amazing insight will be released. Paul spoke about having the gift of prophecy and understanding all mysteries (1 Cor. 13:2). The fullness of understanding will never happen on earth, but it will be released to us once we are outside the body.

Once we are in heaven, we will recognize family, friends, former church members, and anyone else we knew on earth. We will even recognize people we've never met, including those from biblical days.

The question then arises, will we also have knowledge of unregenerate family members who died without Christ and are separated from us in the chambers of hades and sheol? There is little scriptural teaching on this thought, but there are some points to be made regarding how God forgets.

One of the great mysteries of God's nature is His ability to *know all things* and yet *choose to forget* other things. God is omniscient; He designed your body in the womb (Psalms 139:14-16; Jeremiah 1:5), counts the number of your days, and knows all the sins you have committed. Yet, through your confession of sins and repentance, He will place you in a redemptive covenant and forgive and forget those sins. This seems impossible, yet the Bible indicates this does occur: "I, even I, am He who blots out your transgressions for My own sake; and I will not remember your sins" (Isaiah 43:25 NKJV).

The word "remember" in Hebrew is *zakar,* meaning *to mark or make mention of.* Thus, the Lord will never and can never *bring up* any sin that has been forgiven and cleansed by the blood of Christ. God told Jeremiah that if Israel would repent and receive His law in their hearts, He would "forgive them and remember their sins no more" (Jer. 31:34).

We are not certain if God completely erases the memory of your sins from His thoughts, or if He simply refuses to permit your past sins to ever be brought up again. The word *zakar* can allude to not mentioning something. One thing we are certain of is that He forgives, because forgiveness is a reason for the death and resurrection of Christ.

When we stand on the Day of Judgment, we must still have memory of events which transpired on earth. Otherwise, we would have no comprehension of the heavenly record of our deeds when they are presented at the Judgment Seat of Christ. This judgment, called the Bema, occurs in heaven (Rev. 11:18) and is exclusively for those who died in Christ or were living and caught up to be with the Lord (1 Thess. 4:14-17). Paul wrote:

> *"But why do you judge your brother? Or why do you show contempt for your brother? For we shall all stand before the judgment seat of Christ. 'As I live,' says the Lord, 'Every knee shall bow to Me, and every tongue shall confess to God.' So then each of us shall give account of himself to God. Therefore let us not judge one another anymore, but rather resolve this, not to put a stumbling block or a cause to fall in our brother's way."*
>
> — Romans 14:10-13

> *"For we must all appear before the judgment seat of Christ, that each one may receive the things done in the body, according to what he has done, whether good or bad."*
>
> — 2 Corinthians 5:10

This judgment is based on the *good or bad* we did while in our body, meaning when we lived on earth. Paul warns of contempt or disregard toward your fellow believer and how God will judge us for creating a stumbling block for others. Christ also said we will give account for our words, and our own mouth will seal our guilt or justify our actions.

"But I say to you that for every idle word men may speak, they will give account of it in the day of judgment. For by your words you will be justified, and by your words you will be condemned."

– Matthew 12:36-37

These verses indicate that all believers will *remember* people they dealt with on earth, words that were spoken, and the way they treated each person. At the judgment, the books are opened which contain detailed records of words and actions, and each person will be judged from the information in each book. We are not told who compiled these books, but there is a belief that angels are assigned to individuals, and one of their jobs is to record the events of each person's life.

Cornelius, the Italian centurion, feared God, prayed always, and gave charity to the poor. An angel of the Lord came to him and revealed that his prayers and alms (giving) had come up before God as a memorial. This indicates that heavenly records were kept that recorded this man's prayers and charitable contributions. Perhaps this angel was the messenger assigned to the house of Cornelius and was sent from God to reveal to Cornelius that God was noting his faith, prayers, and charitable giving.

When the Lord and two angels showed up at Abraham's tent, they were on a heavenly assignment to prepare Lot for the destruction of the city of Sodom. The two angels, whose appearance was as two human men, were to journey to Sodom and investigate reports coming from the distressing cries of people in the city. We read:

"And the Lord said, "Because the outcry against Sodom and Gomorrah is great, and because their sin is very grave, I will go down now and see whether they have done altogether according to the outcry against it that has come to Me; and if not, I will know.""

– Genesis 18:20-21

The cries of innocent victims and abused individuals ascend to the ears of God, and their cries can move angelic messengers to bring judgment against the abuser. Jesus told us that children have an angel in heaven that continually sees the face of God (Matt. 18:10). He warned against offending a little one and said that, if you are the offender, it would be better to tie a millstone around your neck and drown yourself in the sea.

At the Judgment Seat of Christ, each person being judged will have full recall of past words and actions. The good will be rewarded and the bad can cause a person to lose an eternal reward, including the possibility of losing their crown (Rev. 3:11).

Christ warned His critics and unbelieving enemies that, at the Great White Throne Judgment (Rev. 20:11-15), it will be more tolerable for the wicked men of Sodom than for the religious leaders who mocked and blasphemed (Matt. 10:15; 11:23-24). Christ noted that the men of Nineveh and the queen of the south would testify against Christ's generation, because they saw the Messiah and His miracles and refused to believe (Matt. 12:41-42). This indicates that information dating back thousands of years will be known and revealed at the future judgment. Up to the time of the Great White Throne Judgment, memories of the past will be maintained in the minds of all humans.

WHEN YOUR MEMORY IS ERASED

There is one Scripture that seems to contradict the idea of retaining our earthly memory in heaven: "For, behold, I create new heavens and a new earth; and the former shall not be remembered or come to mind" (Isaiah 65:17 - NKJV).

At the Judgment Seat of Christ (Rev. 11:18), we will have recall of people, places, and events. This will continue as we rule with Christ on earth for a thousand years. The thousand-year reign is followed by the

Great White Throne Judgment (Rev. 20:11-15). Death and hell are cast into the lake of fire; then God creates a new heaven and a new earth (Rev. 21:1). Once the New Jerusalem comes down from God out of heaven, He will dwell with His people, wipe away all tears, and abolish death, sorrow, crying, and pain. Former things pass away, and the Lord will make *all things new* (Rev. 21:1-5).

This is when the *former things* (life on the previous earth) will no longer be remembered. During the thousand-year reign of Christ on earth, all resurrected believers will begin a new life of ruling and reigning with Christ.

When we step into eternal timelessness, I believe one of the reasons past things never enter your mind is to delete the memory of anyone from our bloodline who died without Christ's redemptive covenant. It would not be a joyful future if, for ages to come, our minds were upon those eternally separated from us. Also, life has many disappointments, negative memories, and bad circumstances that need to be erased from our memory.

God gave us memory on earth so that we will be able to recall important and necessary information, and to store images in our brain. Memory serves a practical, but also a spiritual function. It enables us to recall the words, promises, and commandments of God, who continually told Israel to remember the Sabbath (Exod. 20:8); remember all the commandments and do them (Num. 15:39); and remember that the Lord led you (Deut. 8:2), all indicating the necessity of a good memory.

Eventually we will leave this planet. In 2 Peter 1:13-15 (KJV), we read:

> "Yea, I think it meet, as long as I am in this tabernacle, to stir you up by putting you in remembrance; Knowing that shortly I must put off this my tabernacle, even as our Lord Jesus Christ hath showed me. Moreover, I will endeavor that ye may be able after my decease to have these things always in remembrance."

Peter called his physical body "my tabernacle" (verse 14). The word *tabernacle* here is *skenoma* in Greek, and it refers to *a tent*. Paul also used the word tabernacle when referring to the physical body (2 Cor. 5:1, 4). Peter spoke of building three tabernacles during the transfiguration (Matt. 17:4), and he used the word *skenos*. The idea is that, just as a tent is a dwelling place that does not last forever, neither does the physical body last forever.

The "putting off of my tabernacle" referred to Peter's death, which did happen shortly after he wrote this epistle. He desired that, after his death (decease), believers would continue to remember these things. The word decease in Greek is *exodos*, meaning "the road out" or "departure." This word is used in the New Testament when Moses and Elijah spoke of Jesus' death (decease - Luke 9:31), and in Hebrews 11:22 as it refers to the departure of Israel out of Egypt (known as the Exodus). Our death is literally an exodus, similar to the great departure of the Hebrew nation out of Egypt to their Promised Land.

THE MEMORY OF THE SINNER

Luke recorded a story where Christ spoke of a beggar and a rich man, both of whom died about the same time. The rich man found his soul and spirit in hell, but the beggar was carried by angels into Abraham's bosom. In hell, the former rich man could recall his past life and the fact that he had five brothers still living on earth. He wanted them to be warned not to come to this terrible place of fire and confinement. The memory of this selfish man was just as active after death as when he lived on earth.

Sinners and unbelievers who passed from this life and are confined in the chambers of the underworld also maintain their memories while in confinement. At the Great White Throne Judgment, when "death and hell deliver up the dead which are in them" (Rev. 20:13), the memories of their past actions must be recalled. At the judgment, they must answer for the deeds of their life and words of their mouth, and they will be judged according to their works (Rev. 20:12).

After this judgment, death and hell are cast into the lake of fire, a final place of eternal punishment. This is called the "second death" (Rev. 20:14). Some have viewed "second death" to indicate that all those in hell will, at this point, be consumed and annihilated once and for all, thus they will completely perish. When teaching this doctrine, some point out where Christ said that it was not His will that any perish, indicating that, in the end, the sinners in the lake of fire will completely be consumed to ashes and no longer exist.

Consider the condition of the lost soul at this moment. They are in a compartment known as hell. Christ was clear that hell has fire and is a place of torment and punishment (Matt. 5:22; 13:42, 50; Mark 9:43-49). Some souls have been confined in this region for hundreds and even thousands of years. Yet, their spirits and souls still exist and have not been consumed. The lake of fire contains literal fire and this punishment is eternal. This is clear when we read that the devil, the beast, and the false prophet are tormented in the lake of fire, day and night, forever and ever (Rev. 20:10). Simply, forever means forever.

When Christ said that He did not want anyone to perish, the word does not refer to being annihilated. It means to *destroy, to die, or to lose (especially a life)*. When a person dies in a horrible fire, we say they perished in the fire. Christ is indicating that He does not want anyone to experience the second death, or the second separation from Him and our Heavenly Father. The first death was the death of the earthly body, with the soul and spirit being cast into hell. The second death occurs after the day of judgment, with the unbeliever being cast into the lake of fire for eternity.

Scripture is unclear whether the sinner retains memories of life on earth once they are confined in the lake of fire. Our only biblical reference is Luke 16:19-31 where the rich man, while tormented in hell, was aware of his family members on earth.

If I were you, I would ensure my eternal destiny by entering the redemptive covenant with Christ. He alone has provided a plan of escape from eternal death and the way for eternal life. There is nothing appealing about the idea of spending eternity with Satan, his fallen beings, and unrepentant sinners.

CHAPTER 9

WHEN THE DEAD APPEAR IN A DREAM OR VISION

Years ago, one of my wife's dear friends named Kim experienced the unexpected suicide of her elder son. He believed in Christ and truly loved the Lord, but he was battling things that overwhelmed him, and he was gripped by a feeling of hopelessness.

Years later, her younger son and only living child took a pill someone had given him to help him sleep. Unknown to him, it had been laced with fentanyl. On Christmas evening he went to bed, only to be found deceased the next morning. He had battled drug addiction in the past, but he was clean at the time of his death. He was serving the Lord by this time, but one pill took his life.

Kim was a single mother who had now lost her only two children. Her grief in the months that followed was overwhelming.

During our conversation at dinner one evening, Kim's close friend, Kelvin, told us a dream that he had shortly after Kim's younger son, Jacob, died. In this dream, Kelvin was standing on a road that radiated various shades of gold. In the distance he saw Jacob with his hands cupped around his mouth as he called out, "Mom! Mom! Look at me. Look where I am! Here you will be also!" He paused, then repeated the comment. His voice was loud and filled the area where he stood.

When Jacob moved his hands away from his mouth, Kelvin saw

his unique smile. He also noticed a light or illumination coming from inside his spirit and out through his mouth each time he spoke. Jacob looked toward Kelvin, but never spoke to him. He seemed to know that Kelvin had heard the message and would relay it to his mother. It was as though Jacob wanted his mother to know that his eternal spirit was with the Lord, and he was doing great.

SEEING THE DEPARTED

In over four decades of traveling and meeting tens of thousands of Christians from various denominational backgrounds, there is a common question that many have asked. It relates to seeing a deceased loved one in a dream or a vision. On rare occasions, a deceased family member seemed to visibly appear to an individual.

These encounters are soul stirring and often comforting to the family member who was grieving. However, many Christians are afraid to speak about the experience for fear of criticism or mockery. In this chapter I will explain two different encounters that happened to me personally. I will share three true and astonishing stories, then explore these manifestations from a biblical viewpoint.

Tens of thousands of people, at some point, have had a dream or vision of someone who has died. It is not a strange thing to have a dream of someone we love whose spirit is with the Lord. For a Christian, if the loved one shares a warning or instruction, it is simply God's way of revealing information to us through a person we trusted in our lifetime. It does not mean the person left heaven to return to the earth. It could have been a vision similar to those of a biblical prophet, such as Moses or Ezekiel, who saw details of heaven but were living on the earth when the experiences occurred.

THE GREENBRIER "GHOST"

The secular world sometimes refers to these types of manifestations as "seeing a ghost." This is an explanation used by people to describe a spirit of any type which they say they encountered. Secularists have little to no biblical revelation of the spirit world, angels, demons, or the human spirit. Nor do they have a clear understanding of what occurs the moment a person dies.

Along the side of a road just outside of Greenbrier, West Virginia stands a cast iron sign that was posted by the state of West Virginia. The heading, printed in black raised capital letters, reads: GREENBRIER GHOST. The rest of the sign reads:

> *Interred in nearby cemetery is Zona Hester Shue. Her death in 1897 was presumed natural until her spirit appeared to her mother to describe how she was killed by her husband Edward. Autopsy on the exhumed body verified the apparition's account. Edward, found guilty of murder, was sentenced to the state prison. Only known case in which testimony from ghost helped convict a murderer.*

This type of manifestation is strange and often unexplainable. Over my lifetime, I have had two similar experiences that I knew came from the Lord.

MY GRANDMOTHER LUCY BAVA

John and Lucy Bava, our grandparents on my mother's side of the family, were involved with ministry throughout their married lives. Both remained in good health most of their lives and lived to be in their eighties. After my grandfather's death in 1997, my grandmother Lucy moved from her home in West Virginia to Cleveland. She lived with one of her daughters and occasionally came to our office to work in the mail room of our ministry center.

A few months before my grandfather passed away, he called me and said he had an unusual dream. He saw his deceased father, mother, and little brother Tony (who died at a young age) standing together on a beautiful ledge somewhere in heaven. They were beckoning him to come home, which would allude to coming home to heaven. A few months later, Granddad Bava required surgery and passed away while in the hospital.

Before my grandmother departed this life, she told us of a dream she had. She said, "I saw John in a dream. He was in heaven, and he told me, 'Lucy, come here, I want to show you something.'" He took her to a massive and beautiful banquet hall. As far as the eye could see were tables arrayed with bright white tablecloths. Granddad told her that this was the place where the Marriage Supper of the Lamb would take place, and that many people are involved in the heavenly preparations. He pointed to a long table and said, "That is where our family will be sitting."

I sensed that she would be leaving us soon. In October of 2002, my grandmother was taken to a local hospital for emergency surgery. She never left the hospital. In a short time, she went home to be with Christ and the believers who had gone before.

THE STRANGE VISION

A few years after she died, I had a strange experience. This was a vision and not a dream. I had been asleep, when suddenly I was awakened. The master bedroom was usually dark, with only dim natural moonlight slipping through cracks in the window shades. I saw someone standing a few feet from my bed. I sat up slightly and to my astonishment, I saw someone who appeared to be my grandmother Lucy. The best way to describe her was that she looked like a three-dimensional hologram with a slightly clear appearance. She looked young, much the way she appeared in photographs when she was in her twenties or thirties. I could sense that I was seeing her spirit and not her body.

I was expecting her to speak, but she said nothing. Yet, I knew exactly what she was thinking. I understood every thought and unspoken word. There was no "hello" or "how are you." The message she brought was a bit surprising: "Fourteen years from now, you will experience death."

Then she vanished before my eyes. The rest of the night I was restless and could not go back to sleep. I got up and documented the experience, calculating the approximate time when this alleged death would occur.

If this had been a dream, it would not have impacted me as much. However, I had been awake and literally saw someone I knew. I was reminded of Moses who had died, and God had buried him. Yet Moses, along with Elijah, appeared to Christ and three of His disciples in a vision on the Mount of Transfiguration about fifteen hundred years later (Mark 9:4). The discussion was concerning Christ's death and suffering in Jerusalem.

Moses had recorded types and shadows of the Messiah in the Torah. Both Moses and Elijah, former prophets, had received vital information from God that needed to be made known to Christ. All three men conversed as a glory cloud engulfed them. Perhaps the purpose of the glory cloud was to prevent any demonic spirit, or even Satan himself, from hearing the information that was being relayed to Christ. After this happened, Christ never revealed to Peter, James, or John anything that Moses or Elijah had told Him.

FOR FOURTEEN YEARS

At the time, my wife Pam and my father, Fred Stone, were the only people I talked to about this. Pam's comment was, "I guess time will tell what this means." She felt that, if it were a warning, perhaps I should do as King Hezekiah and ask God for an extension of more years. My father was cautious and discerning. When I told him, he said, "Son, this is what you need to be cautious about. The Lord can give you a warning or information in advance. But be careful that a spirit of fear doesn't overcome you, so that you don't open a door for something to happen." He thought it strange that a specific time frame of fourteen years was given.

Ten years later, I reminded Pam that the fourteen-year timeframe was coming up. She thought I should share the experience with our ministry board of directors. They were concerned but questioned if I believed this was from the Lord. The looming question was, "Do you think something will happen?"

I could only reply, "Time will tell."

In that meeting, the board discussed the fact that every ministry needs someone they are either training or preparing to take over the reins if the leader passes. It was discussed that Dr. Bryan Cutshall, a dedicated and gifted minister, trainer, and administrator, would be the person capable of handling the continuation of the ministry. At the time I was overseeing both Voice of Evangelism and Omega Center International, as well as helping to build ISOW, the online Bible school. I was working about fifteen hours a day and barely taking a day off.

I knew that things of this nature must be shared only with close friends who are spiritually minded. However, I made the mistake of telling the vision and death prediction to a few people who did not fall into that category. In the thirteenth year, a couple of those individuals began to ask me, "Do you think something's going to happen to you? Do you think you're going to die soon? Who is taking over if you die?" I began to have a gut feeling that the motivation for asking was to ensure that they would be a significant part of the replacement process.

FOURTEEN YEARS LATER

The fourteenth year from the date of the vision arrived in June of 2020. During this time, I was experiencing the worst satanic assault ever—physically, mentally, and emotionally—from multiple directions.

At a well-respected clinic, a noted physician conducted a battery of tests and determined that I was in such horrible physical condition that, unless I removed stress, slowed down, rested, and changed my fast-paced lifestyle, I would not live long enough to see my daughter get married.

During this time, under the supervision of the ministry board, I stepped aside from all ministry activity for six months. I handed over the ISOW school to the complete leadership of the highly capable Dr. Bryan Cutshall. After seeking God's direction, Omega Center International, which is our main conference center and the location of our Tuesday night services, became the Ramp at OCI, under the direction of Karen Wheaton. Today, Dr. Cutshall leads the Ramp at OCI, including Tuesday services and prayer.

The "death" I was warned about did not turn out to be a *physical death,* although it easily could have been. I had a complete physical burnout and emotional collapse, bringing various problems upon myself. The death was similar to Abraham putting Isaac on the altar and placing his dream of a nation and his prophetic future completely into the hands of God. I learned that, at times, your Isaac gets up from the altar, while at other times, he stays on the altar and you walk away. I died to self and to all my plans. This death reminds me of Paul's words, "I die daily" (1 Cor. 15:31).

Because of the vision years earlier, I knew something was coming and I had, to some extent, mentally prepared myself. God knew what was coming years earlier, and He could have informed me in many ways. However, the appearance of my grandmother in the vision was so dramatic and unusual that it kept my attention for all those years.

We can forget dreams unless we write them down and refer to them often, but it is almost impossible to forget a vision.

A STRANGE DREAM OF MY FATHER

We all occasionally dream of family, some living and some with the Lord. Most of those dreams have little or no spiritual significance. However, any dream with an important warning or meaning will remain with you. Sometimes it will contain unusual symbolism found in Scripture that helps you interpret the meaning of the dream.

My beloved father, Fred Stone, a minister of the Gospel for sixty years, departed this life to be with Christ in March of 2011. In late 2020, while in a deep sleep, I dreamed of seeing my father sitting in a room that appeared to be a small studio that contained video, computers, and recording equipment. He was looking at the screens and listening to someone's recordings. I was behind him observing, when he turned to me and gave me information that related to a few individuals connected to a conflict. His words were encouragement to me. I had the feeling that, although he was in heaven now, he still was aware of things occurring here, and the Lord desired to make me aware of certain events.

In the dream, I left the room and stepped outside onto a sidewalk. Directly in front of me was a river that had flooded, and the water had reached the edge of the sidewalk. The slow-moving water was brown and muddy. I looked in the middle of the river and saw something slowly rising out of the river. It had the appearance of an adult alligator. However, instead of having the leathery skin of an alligator, this one was made entirely of paper and was covered in brown mud from the river. It saw me and began making its way from the water to the shore. I ran from it. Then I realized it was made of paper and represented more of a mental than a physical attack.

The following morning, I told my wife the strange dream and how Dad provided information about certain individuals. I told Pam, "Based on the dream, it appears to be a warning of being "dragged through the mud."" The dream came to pass on two different levels. The warning from my father was true, and during this season it brought me encouragement.

Please do not misunderstand my purpose for sharing this. In none of these instances was I seeking some strange, out-of-this-world visitation. All came as a surprise. In the early church there was a time when people were seeking angelic visitations more than the visitation of the Holy Spirit, which led to angel worship. That is wrong. *First and foremost, our information should be derived from the Holy Bible. Secondarily, it comes from the inspiration and revelation of the Holy Spirit Himself.*

A DECEASED RELATIVE APPEARING TO THE LIVING

Around the world, stories abound of believers having dreams or visions of deceased family members who provided vital information or a warning to the person who was still living. This is more common than some people think. Can a departed soul, one who is presently in paradise, ever return to the earth prior to their resurrection? While I certainly am cautious in attempting to answer this question, I am aware of several individuals, all godly Christians who serve the Lord and engage in prayer and fasting, who experienced an event that absolutely would be termed supernatural.

Bea Ogle, who today is in her early nineties, is one of the most righteous women of God I have ever known. Bea organized and has directed our Daughters of Rachel intercession ministry since 1981, and I have known her since I was eighteen years of age. Bea was married to Elroy Ogle for sixty-four years until he passed away in his eighties, leaving her a widow with no biological children.

Several weeks after Elroy's death, Bea was lying in bed and trying to sleep. She felt an unusual presence enter the room, when suddenly she saw Elroy, dressed in a colorful shirt and looking as he did when he was a young man. He sat on the edge of the bed. She could read his thoughts as clearly as if he were carrying on a conversation. He expressed concern for the condition of the house, apologized for not fixing the roof, and told her what she should do. Then he vanished.

Bea told me, "I was not asleep, nor was I dreaming." She had experienced some type of vision—the same type that the prophets of Scripture experienced when they saw a vision of an angel (see Acts 10:3; 16:9). An angel is a heavenly spirit that is invisible to the natural eyes but can be seen in a vision (see Daniel 8).

A second incident told to me many years ago occurred in Tuscumbia, Alabama. An older man, a strong Christian, told his wife that, if he died before she did, he wanted her to know that he had left her a lot of cash. However, he never told her where his secret stash was hidden.

After he died, his wife needed additional income to pay bills. She had searched through possible hiding places for the cash but found nothing. After praying intently for God's help, one night she awoke from a deep sleep and saw her husband standing at a closet near the bed. He opened the closet door and pointed to a stack of neatly folded quilts on the top shelf. He pointed out a certain one before he smiled and vanished. The room was dark, but she could see him clearly.

She checked the blanket and to her surprise, she found the money concealed between the folds. She never would have thought to look in an old blanket. She was thankful to God for answering her prayer.

One of the most dramatic experiences I ever knew about happened when I was a young boy and my dad was pastoring a church in Big Stone Gap, Virginia. An older couple, the Coopers, lived in Norton,

Virginia and drove each Sunday to attend church. When Mr. Cooper died, his wife no longer could attend church because she lived many miles away and did not drive. Her son helped her move from Norton to a small first floor apartment located next to the church and about sixty feet from our house, which was behind the church.

Her son set a strict monthly budget, instructing her that she could no longer send her monthly donation to Church of God World Missions, but must use that money toward groceries. For decades after they married, she and her husband never missed sending monthly support for world missions. The son advised that her small donation wouldn't make a difference, and that the missions department would not miss her money. She rejected the idea, but her son insisted, since her income was now limited. She complied.

A few weeks later, she was asleep in her small apartment. Suddenly she was awakened by the sound of beautiful singing coming from outside between her first-floor apartment and the church. A bright light was shining through her bedroom window. Thinking she had overslept, she was curious about who was singing. Peeking out from the curtain of her bedroom widow, she observed perhaps forty to fifty people, all dressed in white, standing in several rows on a small hill next to the church. They were singing a beautiful song about redemption that she had never heard before. A man with his back to her was directing this choir.

She observed that these individuals were from different nations. As they continued to sing, the man leading this choir turned toward the window and looked at her. The man was her husband, whom she said now looked to be in his thirties! When he saw her, he and those in the choir blew kisses at her. Then the entire group floated upward, eventually disappearing into the atmosphere. The song and the light faded, and the outside returned to nighttime darkness.

She was so stunned that she immediately called my dad, who was her pastor, and asked him to come quickly to her apartment. Dad thought perhaps she was having a medical emergency. He dressed and ran swiftly across our yard to her apartment, noticing that all the lights were on. When he walked in, she was sitting at her table writing a check for world missions. She told Dad what she had seen and ordered him to mail the check and get it out of her house.

Mrs. Cooper knew that this unusual experience was a sign that their years of giving to world missions had won many souls to Christ. Clearly, it was both God's will and her husband's determination that her giving must continue. A few dollars a month might have seemed small to man, but to God it was a tool for evangelism. It seemed that, in heaven, her husband had met souls who were converted to Christ through their years of giving. God allowed the vision to encourage her and inspire her to continue the monthly support.

THE COMMON THREADS

These three visions have common threads. All three women were widows with no husband or family member living with them to help care for them. Did God allow their husbands to literally return from paradise to appear and bring comfort or information?

Notice that in each case there was no verbal conversation. Bea could read Elroy's thoughts. In the second example, the late husband simply pointed to a location in the closet. No words were shared in the third situation, either. None of these cases involved anyone attempting to contact the dead, which is forbidden in Scripture. Each incident was sovereign, supernatural, and from God.

Also note that, in all three instances, the husbands were advanced in age when they died, but all appeared to be decades younger in the visions. Each woman had been married to her husband for decades. An elderly widow often lives on limited income after the death of her companion, and this would be a cause of concern for any caring and loving companion.

In each case, these three women of great faith believed that the visual appearance of their companion was literal. It was not a figment of their imagination, and they were not hallucinating. They each were awake, thus making this a more vibrant experience.

All three of these appearances *can* be considered a vision. After Moses and Elijah appeared on the Mount of Transfiguration and spoke to Jesus, He told His three disciples to tell nobody the vision (Matt. 17:9).

By biblical measure, a vision is more than just a supernatural manifestation that occurs late at night. It can happen during the day and while fully alert. Note how the women standing at Christ's tomb who *saw* and *spoke* to the angels referred to the experience as a *vision* (see Luke 24:23). In a broad sense, a vision is a moment when the veil is removed from the eyes, thus enabling the visionary to see into the spirit realm for a brief time.

Paul saw a vision at night of an unknown man who asked him to come to Macedonia to preach (Acts 16:9-10). When Zacharias, the father of John the baptizer, saw Gabriel standing at the right side of the golden altar of incense, this older priest departed from the holy place unable to speak. The people "perceived that he had seen a vision in the temple" (Luke 1:22).

Despite examples such as these that bring comfort to people experiencing them, some in the Christian community write this off as demonic. These typically are people who hold to a theology that there is no operation of the miraculous or supernatural in the church today.

Others want a biblical example for such a manifestation. There is a powerful example, as previously noted, in the New Testament.

MOSES SPOKE TO CHRIST PERSONALLY

At the time of Christ's ministry, the prophet Moses had been dead for about 1,500 years. The Bible indicates that he was one hundred and twenty years of age when he died (Deut. 34:5-7). God Himself buried Moses to keep anyone from finding his grave, building a memorial to him, and perhaps worshipping him.

Even though long deceased, Moses visibly appeared with Elijah and was seen by Christ and three of His closest disciples, Peter, James, and John. Moses and Elijah released information directly to Christ concerning His future death in Jerusalem (Luke 9:30-31). God did not resurrect Moses for this special occasion, as there had not been a resurrection of any Old Testament saints as of that time. However, it was the soul and spirit of Moses that appeared.

Moses would have been confined in a location called Abraham's bosom, the same resting place of Abraham and Lazarus (Luke 16). God would have had the spirit of Moses taken from the underworld and allowed him to speak with Christ. Moses, Elijah, and Christ made three, and the law of God says, "In the mouth of two or three witnesses, every word shall be established" (Deut. 19:15; Matt. 18:16). Moses wrote the Torah, and Elijah represented Israel's greatest miracle working prophet. They represented "the law and the prophets" (Luke 16:16).

Four living men—Jesus, Peter, James, and John—were all witnesses to this event. Although the three disciples were not privy to the discussion, they saw both Moses and Elijah, recognizing them through the Spirit of God. Peter later wrote about this event in 2 Peter 1:18: "And this voice which came from heaven we heard, when we were with him in the holy mount."

A FAMILIAR SPIRIT

In the Torah, God made it clear to His people that *attempting to consult the dead* was forbidden. This was a common practice among some pagans, and the instigators of such activity were called mediums, or necromancers (see Deut. 18:10-12). A medium is a person who claims to be a bridge between the physical and the unseen worlds. The word necromancer contains the word necro, which comes from the Greek word *nekros,* meaning, "dead person, corpse, or dead." A necromancer allegedly attempts to contact someone who has died.

Around the nineteenth century, occult activity began to spread in parts of the United States. This included the practice of séances, in which a medium would gather a curious group of people at a table and seek to hear from the spirit of the dead. The medium would allegedly hear something and begin "speaking" on behalf of the departed person. Most of the mediums were exposed as frauds, and the popularity of these gatherings declined.

One reason for God warning His people to never consult and be defiled by a witch, medium, or necromancer (Lev. 19:31; Isa. 8:19) is the danger that a familiar spirit will speak false information, and the naïve and curiosity seeker will be deceived and even led into false teaching. There would be danger of people falling into a trap set by the enemy.

Here is an example. Many years ago, a female minister and friend of our family experienced attacks of the adversary that were impacting her marriage. She took time off with her sister to get away. While on the trip, she met a man who struck up a conversation and said, "I knew I would meet you. I went to a physic who told me I would meet a woman with your color hair who would tell me about God."

Instead of seeing red flags and thinking, "This doesn't sound right because he heard this through a physic," she fell into a trap that eventually led to a divorce because of her contact with this man.

There are various types of spirits mentioned in Scripture. "Familiar spirit" is mentioned seven times in the Old Testament. The familiar spirit would possess and control the medium (or witch), and express words and thoughts to deceive the seekers into thinking their loved one was present and speaking to them.

A familiar spirit has been associated with a geographical location, a person's ancestors, or even crimes that have occurred. Such spirits are able to retain knowledge and information about people and situations. Some of the "ghost hauntings" that we hear about are likely familiar spirits (unless they are staged for television programs).

A familiar spirit is not the spirit of a dead person roaming a house or land for generations, seeking peace or resolution. The soul and spirit of that deceased person is either in paradise with God or confined in the underworld. Instead, it can be a familiar spirit that has been connected to the area for generations.

SPIRITS SEEKING REST

Jesus noted that, when an unclean spirit comes out of a man, it will "walk through dry places seeking rest, and finding none" (Luke 11:24). Once the person they possessed has died, they will roam like a vagabond or seek another person to possess.

This explains how one man mentioned in Mark chapter five, referred to as the man of Gadera, became possessed with two thousand spirits. He lived among the tombs where the dead were buried. In those days people buried the dead right away. If a person who died was possessed by spirits, then the spirit possessing the person could transfer into the man living among the tombs, who was open to receiving those spirits.

There is a difference between seeing a godly, departed loved one in a dream or vision and consulting a medium or necromancer. The person who is *seeking* to contact the other world is breaking the rules and laws of God. In every dream or vision I have experienced or known about, the person was not seeking out the departed soul, nor attempting to make contact. It was a rare and sovereign act of God. In each case, God used the situation to bring a true spiritual warning or a benefit that comforted the individual and brought honor to God.

The idea of having a vision of a righteous loved one is controversial among some Christians. However, remember that God makes the ultimate decision about the things He permits and His purposes for it.

CHAPTER 10

THE MARRIGE SUPPER OF THE LAMB

Not every believer will experience physical death. One day a generation will be alive for the return of Christ, for the event we call the rapture, the catching away, or the gathering together. Those who are alive for this event will be caught up in the clouds to meet the Lord in the air, and they will always be with the Lord, according to Paul in 1 Thessalonians 4:16-17.

After the rapture of the bride of Christ, a much-anticipated event will occur in heaven while the great tribulation events are happening on earth. John wrote about this in Revelation 19:7-9:

> "Let us be glad and rejoice and give Him glory, for the marriage of the Lamb has come, and His wife has made herself ready. And to her it was granted to be arrayed in fine linen, clean and bright, for the fine linen is the righteous acts of the saints. Then he said to me, Write: 'Blessed are those who are called to the marriage supper of the Lamb!' And he said to me, 'These are the true sayings of God.'" (NKJV)

John announced two events in those verses: the marriage of the Lamb and the marriage supper of the Lamb. Paul informed the church at

Corinth that all believers are espoused to one husband (2 Cor. 11:2 KJV). The word espoused can allude to a betrothal, or in modern terms, an engagement between a man and woman.

Paul also indicated that the Holy Spirit is the seal or the earnest of our future inheritance, until the day Christ receives us, His purchased possession (Eph. 1:13-14). The Greek word for earnest is *arrabon,* which refers to the pledge or down-payment for something that will eventually be paid in full. In the context of the church and Christ, the Holy Spirit is the pledge—the engagement ring—that guarantees we are united with and espoused to Him, as we await His arrival to receive us unto Himself (John 14:1-2). We look forward to this magnificent wedding and marriage supper celebration.

The pattern for the wedding is found in ancient Jewish customs. Once the prospective groom paid the pledge to the father of the bride, the young man returned to his hometown and prepared a room on his father's property for himself and his future bride. This is where they would live after marriage. There was no dating, and if she lived in another town, the fellow might not see her again until the day he received approval from his father to go receive his bride. Only the father knew when all things were ready, and the son was obedient to the will of his father. Compare this with the words of Jesus, who said that neither He nor the angels know the day nor hour of His return; only the Father alone knows (Mark 13:32).

In the parable of the ten virgins, the groom had delayed his anticipated arrival to come for his bride. The ten virgins were close friends of the future bride. They were responsible for ensuring that she would remain loyal to the groom, keep her wedding garments clean and white, and keep a lamp trimmed and burning, in case her groom would suddenly appear after sunset.

In the parable, the delay was longer than anticipated, and all ten virgins fell asleep, weary from waiting. Five were prepared with additional oil for their lamps, while five had run out of oil. While the five were searching for oil, the bridegroom arrived and took his bride and the five virgins who had oil in their lamps into the wedding (Matt. 25).

THE KING'S PARABLES

Among the New Testament parables is one found in Luke 14 that alludes to the wedding of a king's son. In this narrative, the king had sent out invitations to his friends to attend his son's wedding. When the day arrived, the king sent messengers to announce that the wedding was prepared. To the king's astonishment, those who received an invitation had made other plans and could not attend the wedding event. The king then sent messengers to the highways and hedges to compel others to attend who normally would not have been invited.

This parable could allude to the fact that Christ came to His own people, yet His own did not receive Him (John 1:11). Therefore, the Gentiles were given the opportunity to be grafted into the New Covenant and will be greatly represented at the marriage supper celebration.

THE HEAVENLY WEDDING AND THE GUESTS

Using the ancient Jewish wedding as our pattern, who are the participants in the heavenly wedding supper?

First is the *Father of the groom*, who is the Almighty God. It will be the wedding of His only begotten son, Jesus Christ, and the Father is the organizer of the event.

The *Bridegroom* is Christ Himself, as indicated in numerous parables. Christ referred to Himself as the bridegroom who would eventually be taken from His disciples (Matt. 9:15). In the parable of the ten virgins, the shout at midnight was, "Behold the bridegroom is coming; go out to meet Him!" (Matt. 25:6).

The bride of Christ is represented by all born again believers who make up the church. They are from all nations, kindred, tongues, and people. Some disagree, pointing out that in John's heavenly vision, he heard a voice saying, "Come, I will show you the bride, the Lamb's wife." John was carried away in the Spirit and saw the city, the New Jerusalem, coming down from heaven, prepared as a bride adorned for her husband (Rev. 21:2-10). However, in the pattern of the Jewish wedding, the New Jerusalem is the *wedding gift*. It is the home that the groom (Christ) prepared for the bride.

Every large Jewish wedding had guests who were invited to participate. This marriage supper is the wedding of the Lamb, referring to the New Covenant that Christ established through His death and resurrection. The guests are also the saints who are part of the first covenant, meaning Abraham, Isaac, Jacob, the sons of Jacob, and the prophets and people from the Old Testament. Christ also noted that Abraham, Isaac, and Jacob would sit down in the kingdom of heaven (Matt. 8:11).

Then there is the "friend of the bridegroom." In a modern wedding, we would call this person "the best man." Typically, the best man is the closest friend of the groom, and he also participates in the wedding ceremony. John the Baptizer was a cousin of Jesus who called himself a friend of the bridegroom:

"John answered and said, 'A man can receive nothing unless it has been given to him from heaven. You yourselves bear me witness, that I said, 'I am not the Christ,' but, 'I have been sent before Him.' He who has the bride is the bridegroom; but the friend of the bridegroom, who stands and hears him, rejoices greatly because of the bridegroom's voice. Therefore, this joy of mine is fulfilled." - John 3:27-29 (NKJV)

Since John was the forerunner to Christ and introduced Him at the Jordan River as the "Lamb of God who takes away the sins of the world" (John 1:27), then John is the "friend of the bridegroom" who will participate as "the best man" who introduces Christ to the bride at His wedding.

John lived and died under the law, which was still in existence prior to the resurrection. The Bible explains that John was the man who served as the transition from the law to grace. Christ noted that, "The law and the prophets were until John. Since that time the kingdom of God has been preached, and everyone is pressing into it" (Luke 16:16).

Every wedding has servants. Christ attended the wedding at Cana of Galilee, where He performed His first miracle of turning water into wine. Mary called for the servants to do whatever Christ instructed them. The servants then prepared six stone water pots, filled them with water, and presented them to Christ (John 2:4-7).

The Greek word here for servants is *diakonos*. This was a person appointed to run errands or to serve at tables; but from a Christian standpoint, the word can also refer to a deacon or deaconess in the early church. In Acts 6:1-5, the apostles selected seven men, full of wisdom and of the Holy Spirit, to "serve tables" and to do the business of the church.

The number of people representing the church age who will be sitting at the tables at the marriage supper will be in the hundreds of millions, perhaps even billions. This will require an unknown, yet large number of servants to serve at the wedding. Some have suggested that those who made it to heaven, but who lost their rewards because of not fully obeying the Lord with their words and actions, might be those who serve at the supper. Others note that angels were created and assigned to minister to men and women during the entire history of the world, and they will be assigned to serve at the supper.

TWO WEDDING WITNESSES

At a Jewish wedding, two witnesses are required. Notice how many times two people are linked throughout Scripture:

- Both Simeon, the aged rabbi, and Anna, a prophetess, were witnesses that the infant Jesus was the Savior (Luke 2:25-39).

- John the Baptist and the Holy Spirit were both witnesses that Christ was the Son of God and Redeemer (Matt. 3:16-17).

- Christ commissioned His disciples to evangelize in groups of two (Luke 10:1).

- In the mouth of two men, Peter and John, the testimony of the empty tomb was received by the others (John 20:1-10).

- Two men (angels) wearing white apparel testified that Christ would return to earth again (Acts 1:10-11).

- At the time of the end, two Old Testament prophets, Elijah and many believe Enoch, will testify that Christ is Messiah during the first half of the seven-year tribulation (Rev. 11:1-3).

- John noted that an invitation was given to all who would hear, saying, "the Spirit and the bride say, Come..." (Rev. 22:17).

Who will be the two witnesses for Christ at His wedding? One must represent the bride and the other, the groom. Paul spoke of espousing the church to one husband (2 Cor. 11:2). Paul would represent the church (the bride), as he wrote at least thirteen New Testament letters to the church (the authorship of Hebrews is debated). He commented that the church would one day be judged by the Gospel he had written (Rom. 2:16; Rom. 16:25). As previously stated, John the Baptizer will represent the bridegroom at the wedding (John 3:28-29).

WHITE LINEN GARMENTS

Throughout the book of Revelation, the common clothing for the martyrs, the saints, and those resurrected from the dead are white robes and white linen garments (Rev. 3:5; 6:11; 7:9). It is noted that the saints will be clothed in fine linen, clean and white (Rev. 19:14).

Linen is one of the oldest kind of fabrics in the world. Biblically, it is mentioned as far back as Joseph in Egypt, and fine linen was worn by royalty (Gen. 41:42). In Exodus 26, the curtains of Moses' tabernacle were dyed in three colors and were all linen. In Exodus 28, the garments of the high priest and the Levitical priests were made of white linen. (Note that the church is also a kingdom of priests who will return with Christ to rule for a thousand years.)

The tabernacle of Moses was in the wilderness where there was much dust. It seems odd that priests wore white linen, especially when considering that blood from a sacrifice would easily stain the white garments. However, the idea is that white represents the righteousness of the saints (Rev. 19:8). Blood was necessary for the remission of sins (Heb. 9:22). Thus, the blood of Christ takes the dark stains of sin and washes the spirit white as snow.

On the wedding day, the bride of Christ will be provided with garments of white. The picture is found in Paul's writings:

> *"Husbands, love your wives, just as Christ also loved the church and gave Himself for her that He might sanctify and cleanse her with the washing of water by the word, that He might present her*

to Himself a glorious church, not having spot or wrinkle or any
such thing, but that she should be holy and without blemish."

— Ephesians 5:25-27

Christ gave Himself for the church, and each believer must prepare himself or herself to be presented to Christ without any guilt or shame. Each person must be faithful to the one who loved you and gave Himself for you!

HEAVEN'S GREATEST ONE YEAR CELEBRATION

Christ's first public miracle occurred at a wedding supper in Cana of Galilee (John 2). His final act in heaven, before returning to earth, will be His own wedding supper.

Among the Jews, the custom was that a marriage supper celebration could last for seven days. This is seen in Judges 14:1-17, where Samson's marriage feast lasted for seven days. Jesus attended the wedding supper in Cana of Galilee. John, the only Gospel writer to record the event, wrote that both Jesus and His disciples were called to the wedding (John 2:2). Some ancient writers believe that this was the wedding of John, who is supposed to have been a near relative of Jesus. It was embarrassing for the head of the wedding supper to run out of food or drink. Mary was concerned, which is a clue that the groom was possibly a relative.

In the Torah, God gave a provision that, when a young man and woman married, they were given one year off work so they could enjoy an extended honeymoon and begin their family (Deut. 24:5). Based on various patterns, it is possible that the heavenly marriage supper occurs at the beginning of the seventh year of the tribulation and continues for one entire year. Every seventh day in a week is a Sabbath where no work is to be done. Every seventh year is a Shemitah year, or a Sabbath year, where the land must rest for one entire year and no farming is done.

FOOD FIT FOR A KING

The heavenly event is a supper, meaning that food will be served. The Greek word for supper can be interpreted as *a dinner, a chief meal, or a feast*. At the Passover supper, also called the "Last Supper," Jesus told His disciples, "I will not anymore eat thereof, until it be fulfilled in the kingdom of God." He added a few moments later, "I appoint unto you a kingdom…that you may eat and drink at my table in my kingdom and sit on thrones judging the twelve tribes of Israel" (Luke 22:29-30).

The meal Jesus is speaking of could be this great marriage supper. His disciples were informed they would sit at His table, which would refer to the head table. The location of this supper will have to be massive, with perhaps millions of tables. It will have to be large enough to house a countless number of individuals from every nation, kindred, and tongue who will be part of the bride of Messiah (Rev. 5:9). When John saw the saints standing before God's throne, mingled with the angels, he said there were "ten thousand times ten thousand and thousands of thousands" (Rev. 5:11).

Scripture does not tell us what kind of food will be served at the Marriage Supper, but we can be certain it will be superb. We do know that there are unique trees in heaven, on either side of the river of life. There also is the tree of life, which bears twelve different types of fruit each month (Rev. 22:2). There are animals in heaven, but since there is no death in heaven, animals will not be slain for food. Like humans, the animals will not experience physical death.

Christ gave a direct word to John about the church at Pergamos, telling them that if they will overcome, in heaven they will "eat of the hidden manna" (Rev. 2:17). Manna was first mentioned during Israel's forty years in the wilderness. It was called "angel's food" and "bread from heaven" (Psa. 78:25 and 105:40). It arrived every morning, six days a week, with double on the sixth day to keep the people from collecting it (and therefore, working) on the Sabbath. The manna was white, the size of a coriander seed, and tasted like wafers made with honey, which would indicate it tasted sweet (Exod. 16:13-18; Num. 11:7). This unusual food could be ground like grain, beaten with a mortar, boiled in a pot, and made into cakes with oil (Num. 11:8). This is the food that sustained over 600,000 men and their families for forty years.

The food at the Marriage Supper may include manna, along with fruits from the various trees. There is no way for us to know for sure what foods will be served, because the Bible is silent. Be assured that, whatever the food, it will be like nothing we have ever eaten on earth. It will be a grand celebration. By the time it concludes, the saints of God will have worshipped before God's throne, participated in the Judgment Seat of Christ, toured all of heaven, and enjoyed the Marriage Supper, where Christ will present the wedding gift to His bride. That gift will be the New Jerusalem, where some believe the mansions (abiding places – John 14:1-4) are waiting.

WHAT DO THE DEAD KNOW PROPHETICALLY?

Even though it is likely the souls of the deceased who dwell in paradise are unaware of earth's time clock, those righteous souls will be alerted when Christ is preparing to return to earth for the resurrection of the dead and the gathering together of the living saints. This is known in 2 Thessalonians 2:1 as the "gathering together" and in 1 Thessalonians 4:16-17 as being "caught up."

Heaven is preparing for the arrival of a massive number of resurrected and living saints. Much activity is occurring there in preparation for the Bema judgment (Rev. 11:18) and the Marriage Supper of the Lamb. Souls of the righteous are involved with these preparations, and they know that the end-time events of which the prophets spoke will occur soon.

A few years ago, I interviewed a pastor named Ronnie Stewart, who told me a dramatic story that revealed activities occurring in paradise. After seeking medical attention for severe weakness, doctors discovered a dangerous staph infection caused by deteriorating pacemaker wires that had pierced the veinous system and the heart itself. Ronnie took antibiotics for a long time, only to later discover that his organs were being infected. He also was informed that he had three near-100% heart blockages. Without surgery he would die, yet with surgery he had only a twenty percent chance of living. He chose surgery at the Texas Medical City in Dallas.

During surgery, he suddenly found himself wide awake and looking to his right. There stood a large angel about eight feet tall and dressed in white. This angel took his spirit by the hand and lifted it out of his body. Now he was able to see the doctor performing surgery on him. Seconds later, he was moving at supersonic speed through the upper realm of space until suddenly, he was standing with the angel by his side in a beautiful courtyard of a large place that seemed to be an arena.

Sitting at a table in the distance were his grandmother, his aunt, and a child who had died fifteen years prior. His aunt was talking to a man and pointing to a beautiful mansion. She was telling the man how surprised she was that it was hers. Ronnie asked the angel the identity of the man. The angel replied, "On earth his name was Anderson, and he was a mentor to your aunt."

After Ronnie returned to his body and recovered from surgery, he gave his testimony on YouTube. A man contacted him to say that he knew who Anderson was. Years ago, the caller had attended Bible school with Ronnie's aunt, and Mr. Anderson was the dean of the college and had spent time mentoring and teaching her. Mr. Anderson had died about a year before Ronnie's heavenly encounter.

The angel then led Ronnie to another arena, similar to a stadium. From the middle of the arena, he looked around and could see two-story mansions. They were covered with beautiful, predominately blue gemstones, and the mortar between them was gold. While in this area he saw his wife's grandmother dancing with a girl who looked to be about ten years of age. He asked the angel, "Who is that girl?" The angel replied, "That is the child she had who was stillborn. She's with her now in heaven."

Ronnie had never heard that she had a stillborn child. When he recovered and was able to speak to his wife, she called her mother and asked if *her* mother had a baby girl who died. The mother said, "It's true. When I was sixteen years old, mom gave birth to a girl who was stillborn, but we never talked about it." Ronnie had seen the little girl in paradise with her mother.

After leaving the area of the gem-studded mansions, the angel took Ronnie to a third fascinating area. Here he saw large, well-constructed stables. In the open fields were countless beautiful, strong horses. One white horse standing close to him wore a breastplate of silver, with writing in a language he couldn't understand. He asked the angel what the writing said, and the angel replied, "In your language it reads, Faithful and True." (This is found in Revelation 19:11.)

Tens of thousands of the horses had riders, and both the horses and riders were wearing armor that was crimson and gold. (Crimson represents blood and gold represents deity.)

One man, who looked like a military general, stood in the front giving instructions. When this man spoke, the horses seemed to understand as much as the riders. They followed his instructions, and sometimes they would rise from the ground or form a circle. Ronnie asked the angel what they were doing. The angel replied, "On earth you would call it military maneuvers. They are preparing for war."

Other horses were doing all the maneuvers, even though they had no riders. When Ronnie asked why there were no riders, the angel replied, "Their riders have not yet arrived."

In the interview, I asked Ronnie if he believed these were the horses referred to in Revelation 19, which the armies of heaven will ride to earth during the battle of Armageddon. He replied that he did believe this is what he saw.

The last thing Ronnie saw before returning to his body was a large room where a man was instructing a group of people. When he asked what the man was teaching, the angel replied, "He is teaching worship to people, young and old, who died without knowing anything about worship." Ronnie understood that some children die before they can ever experience the act of worship, and some people convert to Christ at an older age and die without ever experiencing true worship.

Then the angel told Ronnie, "You are not staying; you are only visiting." Ronnie looked around to find other people he knew who had died. The angel, who could read his thoughts, said to Ronnie, "Just because you do not see them does not mean they are not here."

Ronnie returned to his body in the hospital room, where the doctor was still working on him. After surgery, he was in a coma and on a ventilator for eight days. Even though he could not communicate verbally or see anybody in the room, he knew when his wife and sons were in the room, and he could hear them praying for him.

Notice in Ronnie's heavenly experiences that preparations are being made for future events. Since he was not yet a permanent resident of paradise, his knowledge was limited to information the angel revealed to him, plus knowledge he had on earth.

When souls of the righteous observe the heavenly activities of angels and the preparation for future events, they do not know the exact time of Christ's return. But they are aware that something big is on the horizon!

AFTER THE SUPPER

When the marriage supper concludes, Jesus Christ, the King of kings and Lord of lords, will return to earth with the angels and armies of heaven to take back the earth and seize control of the nations:

> *"Now I saw heaven opened, and behold, a white horse. And He who sat on him was called Faithful and True, and in righteousness He judges and makes war. His eyes were like a flame of fire, and on His head were many crowns. He had a name written that no one knew except Himself. He was clothed with a robe dipped in blood, and His name is called The Word of God. And the armies in heaven, clothed in fine linen, white and clean, followed Him on white horses. Now out of His mouth goes a sharp sword, that with it He should strike the nations. And He Himself will rule them with a rod of iron. He Himself treads the winepress of the fierceness and wrath of Almighty God. And He has on His robe and on His thigh a name written: KING OF KINGS AND LORD OF LORDS."*
>
> — REVELATION 19:11-16 (NKJV)

King Jesus will make war with the antichrist and false prophet and cast them alive into the lake of burning fire. The kings of the earth and their armies who try to make war against Christ and His armies will be killed by His sword that will strike down the nations. Then Christ will reign on the earth for a thousand years (Rev. 20).

CHAPTER 11

RULING AND LIVING IN JERUSALEM FOR A THOUSAND YEARS

The great tribulation will begin on earth with the signing of a treaty (Dan. 9:27). Severe cosmic judgments and natural disasters are initiated from heaven with the breaking of the first seal of a seven-sealed scroll. The scroll will be opened by the Lion of Judah, a title given to Christ (Rev. 5:1-7).

The last day of the great tribulation will not conclude with the all-out destruction of mankind, as some suggest. It will conclude with the stunning, visible return of Christ, who shall destroy His earthy enemies with the brightness of His coming (2 Thess. 2:8). Christ predicted that without His supernatural intervention at the battle of Armageddon—the final war in the Valley of Megiddo in Israel (Rev. 16:16)—no flesh would be saved (Mark 13:20). Christ's sudden coming prevents a weapons of mass destruction type conflict that would wipe out the entire human population.

On the last day of the tribulation, King Jesus will saddle up and return to the Holy City of Jerusalem to rebuild the city and construct a new temple. He will direct a Zadok priesthood and initiate an earthly political and spiritual kingdom, ruled by a theocracy of one—Jesus, the

King of kings and Lord of lords (Rev. 19).

Revelation chapters 19 and 20 reveal truths that, at times, are contrary to traditional beliefs. For example, when I was growing up, I was told that if I received Christ, I would be with Him forever in heaven. Many Gospel songs also express this idea. The fact is, Christ is not going to be *forever* in heaven, and neither are we. Once He transfers from His heavenly position of High Priest to His earthly position of King, Jesus Christ will rule on earth for one thousand years. Then, throughout eternity, He will rule from the center of the city called New Jerusalem that will descend from heaven to earth.

When the global military coalition of the antichrist and his armies on earth have surrounded Israel and Jerusalem at the end of the tribulation, the believers in heaven will return to earth with Christ. The armies in heaven will form what I refer to as God's military alliance. John penned this in his vision of the apocalypse:

> *"Now I saw heaven opened, and behold, a white horse. And He who sat on him was called Faithful and True, and in righteousness He judges and makes war. His eyes were like a flame of fire, and on His head were many crowns. He had a name written that no one knew except Himself. He was clothed with a robe dipped in blood, and His name is called The Word of God. And the armies in heaven, clothed in fine linen, white and clean, followed Him on white horses. Now out of His mouth goes a sharp sword, that with it He should strike the nations. And He Himself will rule them with a rod of iron. He Himself treads the winepress of the fierceness and wrath of Almighty God. And He has on His robe and on His thigh a name written: King of kings and Lord of lords."*
>
> — Revelation 19:11-16 (NKJV)

THE RETURN – THE KING, THE ARMY, AND THE SAINTS

The armies in heaven are a combination of warring angels and saints of God. We know this by comparing other Scriptures that speak of Christ's return. Jude 14 says that the Lord is coming "with ten thousands of his saints, to execute judgment upon all...."

The army has three assignments. The first is to assist Christ in His military campaign to destroy the earth's armies that are attempting to destroy Israel and Jerusalem. Paul wrote that these armies will be destroyed with the brightness of Christ's coming (2 Thess. 2:8).

Christ then will send angels to separate the wheat from the tares, meaning the children of the kingdom from the children of Satan (Matt. 13:36-42). The tares are sent into the fire and the wheat is gathered into the kingdom. The tares are those who practiced lawlessness and received the mark of the beast, and the wheat are those who refused the mark and somehow managed to survive until Christ's return.

The third assignment of the angels will be to gather the Jewish remnant that is scattered across the four regions of the earth. The event will begin with the sounding of a great shofar (Matt. 24:31). This second remnant of Jewish tribulation survivors are considered the elect and will be brought to Jerusalem to rule from the Holy City with the Messiah. Isaiah first wrote of this return:

> "And it shall come to pass in that day, that the great trumpet shall be blown, and they shall come which were ready to perish in the land of Assyria, and the outcasts in the land of Egypt, and shall worship the LORD in the holy mount at Jerusalem."
>
> – ISAIAH 27:13 (KJV)

THE DEVIL'S THOUSAND-YEAR SENTENCING

Satan's doom and imprisonment was predicted around AD 95. John saw an angel descending from heaven and holding a chain and a key (which could represent authority). This angel put Satan under arrest, bound him in chains, and cast him into the bottomless pit for a thousand years (Rev. 20:1-3). The ringleader of the world's accusations and lies will find himself bound in a dark prison, all to himself.

In a fully resurrected body, the saints arriving in Christ's army may be permitted to watch the binding of their archenemy. This is indicated in Isaiah, who wrote about the fall of Lucifer—another name for Satan—and predicted the reaction from people who will see him:

> *"Yet thou shalt be brought down to hell, to the sides of the pit. They that see thee shall narrowly look upon thee, and consider thee, saying, Is this the man that made the earth to tremble, that did shake kingdoms; That made the world as a wilderness, and destroyed the cities thereof; that opened not the house of his prisoners?"*
>
> – ISAIAH 14:15-17 (KJV)

We don't know exactly what Satan looks like. Some imagine him with bright red skin and horns on his head, which is not factual. Others see him as a tall beast covered with layers of bulked up muscles that he flexes to intimidate his enemies. But the reality is that, when we see him bound and headed for a thousand-year prison sentence, we will say, "That's him? He's the one who caused all this trouble?"

The phrase *bottomless pit* is mentioned seven times, all in the book of Revelation (Rev. chapters 9, 11, 17 and 20). The phrase comes from the Greek word *abussos*, which refers to a place that is described by the ancient Greeks as the "infernal regions."

Originally, the word was used to describe the lower underworld that was divided into two parts. In Greek, this was a prison where the mythological gods locked up their enemies. The location became known as tartarus. This is the Greek word that Peter used (2 Peter 2:4) when speaking of the fallen angels that God has bound in chains of darkness in hell. The Greek belief was that this chamber was located beneath the foundations of the mountains of the earth.

In the Torah, when God spoke of fire burning in the lowest hell, He also said it would "set on fire the foundations of the mountains" (Deut. 32:22). The prophet Jonah was thrown overboard from a ship in a storm and swallowed by a great fish. Jonah drowned, as sea weeds wrapped around his head and his soul fainted (Jon. 2:5). The fish preserved his body until God raised him on the third day. Jonah spoke of his journey into the underworld of the departed when he wrote, "I went down to the bottoms of the mountains; the earth with her bars was about me forever" (Jonah 2:6).

Satan will be restrained and confined under the foundations of the mountains, meaning under the crust of the earth, which is twenty-five miles deep. The three times that the Greek word *chain* is used in the New Testament, it refers to someone being bound by chains in prison (Acts 28:20; 2 Tim. 1:16; Rev. 20:1).

An angel places a seal upon Satan to shut him up, thus preventing him from deceiving the nations (Rev. 20:3). The word *seal* has various meanings in the New Testament. God Himself has certain types of seals (John 3:33; Rom. 4:11; 2 Tim. 2:19). The phrase "shut up" primarily refers to a door being shut (Matt. 6:6; Luke 11:7; Rev. 3:8).

The seal is placed upon Satan, and not on the opening of the physical abyss. His deception stems from his voice and his words. Imagine Satan having a seal over his mouth so that he cannot speak. A thousand years is a long time to not speak.

THE KIDRON VALLEY JUDGMENT

The next event to unfold will be the judgment of the nations in Jerusalem. The prediction and imagery of this is concealed in the parable of the separation of the sheep and the goats:

> *"And before him shall be gathered all nations: and he shall separate them one from another, as a shepherd divides his sheep from the goats: And he shall set the sheep on his right hand, but the goats on the left."*
>
> — MATTHEW 25:32-33

The wheat is gathered into the barns, while the tares—those who practice lawlessness and cause someone else to stumble—are separated and burned in the fire (Matt. 13:40). The wheat represents the children of God's kingdom, and the tares are the children of Satan's kingdom of darkness (Matt. 13:38).

This judgment will take place in Jerusalem, in the area that the prophet Joel identified as the valley of Jehoshaphat. Joel 3:12 reads, "Let the heathen be wakened, and come up to the valley of Jehoshaphat; for there will I sit to judge all the heathen round about."

This valley begins at the base of the Mount of Olives and extends to the eastern side of the city of Jerusalem. The valley was known in both Christ's day and in our time as the Kidron Valley. At Christ's return, the Mount of Olives will split. Half will go north and half south, forming a great valley (Zech. 14:4). This will create a large, natural opening where this judgment can occur.

God will gather all nations and separate them, as a shepherd separates the sheep and goats (Matt. 25:32). The sheep will be on His right hand, and the goats on His left. To those on His right, He will say, "Come, you blessed of My Father, inherit the kingdom prepared for you from the foundation of the world" (Matt. 25:34). Scripture identifies the sheep as those who clothed the naked, visited the sick and the imprisoned, and gave water to the thirsty (Matt. 25:35-40).

To the goats on the left He will say, "Depart from Me, you cursed, into the everlasting fire prepared for the devil and his angels" (Matt. 25:41). The goats are identified as those who gave no food, drink, clothes, shelter, or hospitality to the poor, hungry, and imprisoned (Matt. 25:42-45).

The goats on the left will go away into everlasting punishment; the righteous on the right will go into eternal life (Matt. 25:46).

The resurrected and raptured saints already have been judged and received their crowns and rewards in heaven, and they will now rule the earth in Christ's kingdom. Those who survived the tribulation will be judged in Jerusalem. The sheep nations that remain on earth must completely submit to the leadership of Christ.

WHAT WILL WE BE DOING?

One of the common questions I am asked is: What will we be doing during the thousand-year reign, and who are the people living on earth during that time?

During the tribulation, the earth will go through severe destruction, such as never was since there was a nation (Dan. 12:1). Asteroids will destroy land and cause one-third of the waters to become bitter (Rev. 8:10-11). Volcanoes (burning mountains) will erupt, and tsunamis will destroy a third of sea creatures and ships (Rev. 8:8-9). A massive global earthquake, the worst in history, will cause cities of the nations to fall (Rev. 16:18-19).

Any major disaster is always followed by a lengthy clean up. With cities and nations in chaos, it will likely take years to clean up the rubble and rebuild homes and other facilities. During that time there also will be new inventions for communications, transportation, and so on.

The prophet Ezekiel gave a prediction that the Dead Sea, which has no marine life due to its heavy mineral and salt content, will be healed with water that comes from underground aquafers in Jerusalem. Ezekiel saw a thriving fishing industry at the revived Dead Sea, with fish of many kinds that will live in the upper section of the waters (Ezek. 47). Fresh water springs and once hidden underground rivers will emerge, turning the dry desert into a prosperous agricultural center that provides food, not only for the inhabitants of Israel, but for the nations as well. They will fill the world with fruit (Isa. 27:6).

A new economic and monetary policy will be established. Presently, Israel's currency is called the shekel. Throughout the Old Testament, the shekel was a measure of weight used for weighing grains and precious metals. Ezekiel mentions the shekel being used at the Messiah's temple (Ezek. 45:12).

BUILDING THE NEW TEMPLE

Ezekiel received a stunning vision of a future third temple being built where two previous Jewish temples once stood. In the previous temples, God came down once a year on the Day of Atonement to sit between the wings of the cherubim in the Holy of Holies. The third temple will be the earthly home of Christ. It will be His personal residence, and tens of thousands of ministers (priests) will assist during the one-thousand-year reign. It is unknown how long it will take to build this temple. The builders likely will be a combination of saints and tribulation survivors.

It is possible that the saints who have returned with Christ and are ruling with Him from Jerusalem will participate in the preparation and construction of this magnificent worship center. One of the puzzling prophecies in Ezekiel deals with the return of an animal sacrificial system at this temple. Many have lampooned this idea, as Christ's sacrifice was final and complete. According to the book of Hebrews, the animal sacrificial system is now null and void.

However, there is a practical aspect for this prophecy. In Moses' tabernacle and the two Jerusalem temples, the meat and drink offerings presented by the people were used to feed and sustain the many priests, because the Levitical priests were not given a land allotment as were other tribes. The Levitical priests lived off the five different types of offerings that the people provided.

There will again be thousands of ministers and priests (called the sons of Zadok) ministering daily in this temple, which will be the center—the headquarters—of all global spiritual activity. The meat from these memorial offerings will be used to feed thousands of priests and ministers. Ezekiel indicates that there will be numerous slaughter-houses within the new temple compound, and a large altar for burnt offerings.

In addition to being the spiritual center, Jerusalem will become the geopolitical center, with Christ as King and the twelve apostles sitting with Christ and serving as judges (Luke 22:30). With multiplied millions of saints living in the area that is now Israel, the border of Israel will be greatly expanded. The new borders will include all the land that God originally promised to Abraham, from the river of Egypt (the Nile) to the great river Euphrates (Gen. 15:18). Both rivers were originally part of a four-river source that once formed the boundaries of the Garden of Eden (Gen. 2:10-14).

This new and expanded border will be divided equally between the twelve original tribes of Israel, with Jerusalem as the center. The property is divided from east to west, beginning with Dan in the north and extending south to tribe of Gad (Ezek. 48). This expansion is detailed by Ezekiel (47:13-23; 48:1-8). He also noted that strangers (non-Jews) would also be given a special land allotment, and anyone having children in Israel would be given an inheritance in the land (Ezek. 48:22-23).

REPOPULATION OF THE PLANET

After the universal flood of Noah, his three sons settled in three different areas of the earth, later known as Northern Africa, the Middle East, and Asia. Their children and their descendants repopulated the earth. God told Adam and Noah to "*replenish* the earth" (Gen. 1:28; 9:1), a word meaning to fill again—in this case, to procreate and fill with people.

After 4,500 years, from Noah's three sons to the present day, the earth's population is around eight billion people, not including all who have lived and died. By the conclusion of Christ's thousand-year reign, the earth's population should increase dramatically. People will live longer, as it will be a rare thing for people who are born during that time to die before they reach one hundred years of age. Isaiah tells us:

> "*No more shall an infant from there live but a few days,*
> *Nor an old man who has not fulfilled his days;*
> *For the child shall die one hundred years old,*
> *But the sinner being one hundred years old shall be accursed.*"
>
> – Isaiah 65:20 (NKJV)

During the millennial rule of Christ's kingdom, the population will be a mixture of saints with glorified bodies and humans who survived the tribulation. The tribulation survivors eventually will die. Somehow these men and women managed to survive the tribulation judgments and not take the mark of the beast. Some may have survived by living in dens of the earth and caves (Rev. 6:15).

The saints with new bodies will have no ability to procreate, as they will be like the angels, "neither married nor given in marriage" (Matt. 22:30). Those who populate the earth will be the men and women on earth who survived the tribulation and will marry and have children. The number of deaths caused by tribulation events will cause the ratio of women to men to be seven women to one man (Isa. 4:1).

The earth's population will increase slowly, then expand exponentially throughout the thousand years. This repopulation of the earth is reminiscent of the time when Noah and his family survived the global flood, left the ark, and repopulated the earth.

ANOTHER RESURRECTION OF THE DEAD

The armies in heaven, riding with Christ on white horses, will include massive numbers of saints raised from the dead, along with those living who were caught up at the event theologians term *the rapture*. In this army are the dead in Christ who rose first (1 Thess. 4:16) when Christ returned to gather the living and the dead and bring them to heaven. Those who died as martyrs by beheading during the tribulation need be resurrected from the dead to rule with Christ:

> "...*And I saw the souls of those who had been beheaded for their witness to Jesus and for the word of God, who had not worshiped the beast or his image, and had not received his mark on their foreheads or on their hands. And they lived and reigned with Christ for a thousand years. But the rest of the dead did not live again until the thousand years were finished.*"
>
> — REVELATION 20:4-5 (NKJV)

These souls are those alluded to in the early part of the tribulation. They are those who are under the altar of God, waiting until all their fellow servants of Christ are slain by beheading. While living on earth, they refused to receive the mark of the beast or engage in idolatry by worshipping the image (icon is the Greek word) of the beast. These souls are resurrected from the dead at the conclusion of the seven-year tribulation. They are referred to in Daniel 12 when he spoke of God delivering His people during the terrible tribulation, whose names are in the book (of life). Daniel also noted that, "Many of them that sleep in the dust of the earth shall awake...." (Dan. 12:1-2).

Because of the faithfulness of this multitude who did not deny Christ and God's word, and instead became willing to die for their faith, Christ honors their ultimate sacrifice by raising them in a new body and permitting them to rule with Him during the thousand years. John said, "This is the first resurrection" (Rev. 20:5).

However, there was a previous resurrection of the "dead in Christ" the moment Christ returned for the church and changed the living from mortality to immortality. This would have been the first resurrection. Is there a contradiction? Not when you consider that He is speaking here of the martyrs who were waiting in heaven for *their* resurrection. Revelation 20:5 is the first resurrection of the *tribulation* martyrs. There will be several orders of resurrections in the future (1 Cor. 15:23).

John pointed out that "the rest of the dead did not live again until the thousand years were finished" (Rev. 20:5). The rest of the dead John referred to would be those souls in hell that will be resurrected to appear at the Great White Throne Judgment, and the souls of those who died during Christ's thousand-year reign who must also be judged. Angels will also be judged, including the fallen angels (1 Cor. 6:3).

After Satan is bound, John observed, "I saw thrones, and they that sat upon them, and judgment was given to them" (Rev. 20:4). The prophet Daniel experienced a vision in which he saw the saints sitting on thrones and serving as judges.

Daniel saw the Ancient of Days, a term used for the Almighty God. His throne was seen as a flame of fire. His garments were white, and his hair was solid white, with an appearance like wool. There was also a stream of fire coming forth from Him, and ten thousand times ten thousand stood before Him (Dan. 7:9-10). "Ten thousand times ten thousand" is the same phrase used by John when he observed the massive number of individuals worshipping God before His heavenly throne (Rev. 5:11).

Daniel then said, "The judgment was set and the books were opened" (Dan. 7:10). This judgment could be the Judgment Seat of Christ, as the throne is seen as a fiery color. The final judgment occurs at the conclusion of the thousand-year reign.

WHERE WILL YOU LIVE AND WORK?

Most of the Old Testament patriarchs and prophets once lived somewhere in Israel, Judea, or Jerusalem. For over 1,900 years, most followers of Christ have lived in certain Gentile nations, the Western Hemisphere, and even in Eastern Asian nations, some of which persecute believers. The answer to where you will live during the millennial reign will be determined by your assignment.

The parables of Christ contain some insight. A faithful servant will be made ruler over the Lord's goods (Matt. 24:47). Christ indicated that if you were faithful in a few things, He will make you ruler over many things (Matt. 25:23).

What or whom would we rule over? In the parable of the nobleman who left his estate in the hands of his servants, those who were faithful were rewarded. Christ spoke of one who was given ten cities, while a second servant was given five cities. The third servant was afraid to invest the Lord's money and did nothing worthwhile to assist in the growth of what he was assigned to. This third servant received nothing, and what he had been given was taken away and given to the servant with ten cities. In this parable, Christ indicated that those who did the most with what they were given will receive more, and those who did nothing will lose what they had (Luke 19:12-28).

In the millennium, those who were faithful to Christ and His church in their earthly life will rule over nations, towns, and cities. Some will be involved in teaching those who are living on the earth. Some will serve as judges and civic leaders. Others will help with worship at the temple. My wife loves to cook and prepare food, as this is a joy for her. She would be happy to be a chef. Great celebrations, including the yearly Festival of Tabernacles, will be conducted and bring huge crowds to Jerusalem:

> *"And it shall come to pass, that every one that is left of all the nations which came against Jerusalem shall even go up from year to year to worship the King, the LORD of hosts, and to keep the feast of tabernacles."*
>
> — ZECHARIAH 14:16 (KJV)

WHERE WE ONCE LIVED

Since April 1982, the month Pam and I married, we have lived in the same town in Tennessee. For us, this is home. It seems strange to imagine that after returning to earth, we may have new positions and live in a different location.

When I was growing up, my father was a pastor, and our family moved several times. We moved to Southwestern Virginia when I was three, then moved to Northern Virginia, and at age fifteen, moved further south in Virginia. Each move was an adjustment with new places, a new school, a new church, and new friends. But eventually each move felt like home.

In the millennium, you might not be as connected to a familiar place or an old homestead or property the way you are today, as the earth will have undergone cataclysmic changes. Any home or property that is unoccupied during the tribulation will be broken into and everything stolen. Natural disasters might destroy the property. However, in heaven there will be no concern about those earthly treasures, as we have laid up eternal treasures. We set our affections on things above and not on earthly belongings. One fire can burn up everything you own, and one F5 tornado can blow everything away.

Our reward will not be based on our earthly fame or reputation. It will not be based on our income, investments, or possessions. The rewards that we carry from heaven back to earth will be our crowns, our assigned positions, and our authority over cities and nations. This is earned through our obedience and faithfulness to God in this life. We must do His will on earth, and keep our eyes on the souls, the crown, and eternity.

CHAPTER 12

MYSTERIES OF THE NEW JERUSALEM

An interesting verse reveals something few people know about Abraham. While he was journeying throughout the Promised Land, we read, "For he looked for a city which has foundations, whose builder and maker is God" (Heb. 11:10). The Holy City is in heaven and is called "the New Jerusalem." It has existed from ages past, when God created the heavens and the earth.

Jesus said in John 14:2 that "in my Father's house *are* many mansions" (abiding places). He spoke this around the year 32. Notice that the dwelling places were already in existence. In the next verse, Jesus said He was going to "prepare a place," which has been interpreted in sermons and songs as "preparing a mansion." The word *place* in Greek is *topos*, and it refers to a spot, a location, or even a condition or opportunity. Through Christ's death and resurrection, He gave us direct access to God in prayer for forgiveness of sins and future access to dwell in the New Jerusalem.

THE GEMSTONE STUDDED CITY

The New Jerusalem is a city built with precious and semi-precious gemstones. Earth itself is one big gemstone mine for the same stones found on the walls of the New Jerusalem.

163

Before Satan rebelled, we read that he "walked up and down in the midst of the stones of fire" (Ezek. 28:14, 16). I have researched Ezekiel's statements and believe this could have been when the New Jerusalem was being constructed in heaven.

A 1953 Hebrew commentary of Umberto Cassuto's Masoretic text, published by A. S. Hartom, translates "stones of fire" as "sparkling stones" (in modern Hebrew), referring to *gemstones* which have been cut. The Ezekiel verse in the Cambridge Bible (1970) reads, "I will set you as a towering cherub as guardian; you were on God's holy hill and you walked proudly among the stones that flashed like fire." Thus, these stones of fire were not burning rocks, but the formation of gemstones to be used for some purpose in heaven.

Years ago, I ministered in Texas where the pastor once worked with gemstones. Pastor Gary and I discussed how gemstones were created in the earth and how different types of stones are found on different continents. For example, tanzanite is found in Tanzania, Africa, and most of the world's tanzanite mines are there. Diamonds are found in various nations, but the best come from South Africa or Liberia. Emeralds are a precious and valuable gemstone, and the best quality are mined in South America. The finest blue sapphires are mined primarily in Sri Lanka. The sapphire is one of the sacred stones in the Bible, and it is mentioned in twelve verses in both the Old and New Testaments.

Regardless of where these stones are mined, all have one thing in common: they are created out of intense heat and fire.

In John's apocalyptic vision, he saw the New Jerusalem and recorded details of this extraordinary future home for the righteous. He even told us the names of the gemstones that form the walls. On top of the bottom foundation are eleven other levels, and the stones for each level are:

The Gemstone	The 12 Levels
• Jasper	Foundation (Rev. 21:19)
• Sapphire	Second level (Rev. 21:19)
• Chalcedony	Third level (Rev. 21:19)
• Emerald	Fourth level (Rev. 21:19)
• Sardonyx	Fifth level (Rev. 21:20)
• Sardius	Sixth level (Rev. 21:20)
• Chrysolite	Seventh level (Rev. 21:20)
• Beryl	Eighth level (Rev. 21:20)
• Topaz	Ninth level (Rev. 21:20)
• Chrysoprasus	Tenth level (Rev. 21:20)
• Jacinth (Diamond)	Eleventh level (Rev. 21:20)
• Amethyst	Twelfth level (Rev. 21:20)

Genesis chapters 29 and 30 give a list of eleven sons of Jacob (Benjamin came later). One type of gemstone represents each of the twelve sons.

The Name of the Son	The Order of His Birth
• Reuben	His first son (Gen. 29:32)
• Simeon	His second son (Gen. 29:33)

• Levi	His third son (Gen. 29:34)
• Judah	His fourth son (Gen. 29:35)
• Dan	His fifth son (Gen. 30:6)
• Naphtali	His sixth son (Gen. 30:8)
• Gad	His seventh son (Gen. 30:11)
• Asher	His eighth son (Gen. 30:13)
• Issachar	His ninth son (Gen. 30:18)
• Zebulon	His tenth son (Gen. 30:20)
• Joseph	His eleventh son (Gen. 30:24)
• Benjamin	This twelfth son (Gen. Gen. 35:18)

Many years after the patriarch Jacob's death, God instructed Moses to build a sacred tabernacle and organize a priesthood of men from the tribe of Levi. One man would be appointed the high priest and wear special garments reserved only for him. Hanging from two chains on the outer garment of the high priest was a gold breastplate with twelve gemstones. On each stone was carved a name of each of the tribes. These stones represented Jacob's twelve sons. Here is a list of the stones and the son they represented:

The Precious Gemstone	The Son It Represents
Sardis - (Exod. 28:17)	Reuben

Topaz - (Exod. 28:17)	Simeon
Carbuncle - (Exod. 28:17)	Levi
Emerald - (Exod. 28:18)	Judah
Sapphire - (Exod. 28:18)	Dan
Diamond - (Ezek. 28:18)	Naphtali
Ligure - (Exod. 28:19)	Gad
Agate - (Exod. 28:19)	Asher
Amethyst - (Exod. 28:19)	Issachar
Beryl - (Exod. 28:20)	Zebulon
Onyx - (Exod. 28:20)	Joseph
Jasper - (Exod. 28:20)	Benjamin

The beautiful city has a wall of twelve colorful gemstones and twelve gates—three at each cardinal entrance (North, South, East, and West). The gates, made of a solid pearl, are guarded by twelve angels, and the names of the twelve tribes of Israel are carved on the gates. The massive city called New Jerusalem is generally assumed to be a giant cube that is 1,500 miles in width, length, and height.

All this information is confirmed in Revelation 21, except for that which is *assumed*—that the Holy City is shaped like a cube. Some think the New Jerusalem may be shaped like a *pyramid* and not a cube.

The most recognized pyramid shape is that of the famous pyramids in Egypt, some constructed over 4,500 years ago. The creation of Adam dates back on our known chronology to around 6,000 years;

thus, the concept of the pyramid shape could have been known or used sometime prior to the flood of Noah, which occurred 1,656 years from Adam.

Much speculation surrounds the origin of the pyramid shape and the question of who supervised the building of the Egyptian pyramids. Those pyramids are large, triangular-shaped tombs made of rock that housed the mummified bodies of Egyptian pharaohs and their family members, along with some of their wealth. The pyramids have a four-sided square base, with each base rising at an angle to form a four-sided triangle that narrows to a point at the top.

With the enormous size of many pyramid stones, it is possible that the race of giants who once lived on the earth (Gen. 6:4) were involved in the physical building process. These giants still would have been on the earth, particularly in the Middle East, at the time of the pyramid construction.

Before and even after the flood, there was a population of giants on earth who lived in and around the Promised Land (Gen. 6:1-4, Num. 13:33, Duet. 2:10-11, Deut. 3:1). The last of the giants mentioned in Scripture—five of them, including Goliath—were slain in Israel by David and his mighty men (1 Sam. 17:4-7; 1 Chron. 20:3-8).

According to Genesis 6:4 and numerous Jewish sources, such as the *Book of Jubilees*, the *Jewish Talmud*, the *Book of Enoch,* and *Josephus*, these giants were offspring of angels who took on human form and cohabitated with earthly women. These strange facts are also con-firmed in the writings of numerous early church fathers, including Justin Martyr and Clement of Alexander.

Various early church fathers pointed out that these fallen angels and giants were the basis for the corrupt mythology among the Greek poets and philosophers. This idea of giants being the offspring of fallen angels was believed in the time of Christ. It was changed in the fourth century by Julius Africanus (see *Wilmington's Guide to the Bible - Fallen Angels and Giants - page 25*).

Being the biological offspring of the sons of God and the daughters of men, some in that day viewed them as part god and part man. The ancient Sumerians, a people group living in ancient Mesopotamia, believed that these "star gods" must be worshipped on mountain peaks. If they did not have mountains, they built them. (Satan and his angels once worshipped on the holy mountain in heaven). People in early times were fully aware of these so-called demi-gods, and they wrote about them in ancient records.

At times, angels are identified as *strangers* who can be entertained unwittingly, meaning they can manifest as humans, and those around them are unaware that they are angels (Heb. 13:2). Some teach that it is the angels who participated in procreation with humans (Gen. 6:4) and were removed from earth at some point and labeled fallen angels, who are now bound in tartarus (hell) under the earth (2 Pet. 2:4). These angels once had been in heaven, in the heavenly temple of God. They would have seen the construction of the New Jerusalem, in ages past, which brings us back to the original thought: the shape of the New Jerusalem.

NOT NECESSARILY A CUBE

From the time I was a child, every minister who described the New Jerusalem would talk about the foursquare city, giving the listener a visual of a cube-shaped Holy City. However, carefully read John's description in Revelation 21:16-17 (NKJV):

> *"The city is laid out as a square; its length is as great as its breadth. And he measured the city with the reed: twelve thousand furlongs. Its length, breadth, and height are equal. Then he measured its wall: one hundred and forty-four cubits, according to the measure of a man, that is, of an angel."*

John doesn't describe the city as cubical, or a 1,500-hundred-mile square shape. He wrote that the city's foundation is laid out in a square pattern of 12 thousand furlongs, which translates to about 1,500-hundred-miles square, laying out the foundation north to south and east to west. The length and width are equal to the height; meaning from the base to top is also 12 thousand furlongs, or 1,500 miles high. It has been *assumed* that the city is cubical.

However, the New Jerusalem could be shaped like the pyramids in Egypt, except that the New Jerusalem is exceedingly enormous and luxurious—more so than anything ever built on earth. Picture four sides, each 1,500 miles in length at the foundation level, with a triangular-shaped wall rising 1,500 miles from each side of the foundation. The four outer walls would slant and rise to a peak at the top.

The fact that there are four directions—north, south, east, and west—means that the square pyramid base would be the shape of the brass altar and golden altar, both with four "horns" on the four corners, representing the four directions of the earth.

THE GREAT PYRAMID IN GIZA

An unusual man-made structure and the only one of the Seven Wonders of the Ancient World that remains is the Great Pyramid of Giza in Egypt. It was built during the reign of Khufu, between 2589 and 2566 BCE. The pyramid rises to about 480 feet with four equal sides, and it was once the tallest man-made structure in the world.

The 5.75-million-ton Great Pyramid was constructed with about 2.3 million stones, with weight estimations ranging from 2.75 tons to fifty tons per stone. The corners at the base of the pyramid align with the four points of a compass—north, south, east, and west. With its size, design, and the weight of each stone, even Egyptologists and archeologists are uncertain how it was built.

Another mystery is the type of mortar that was used because it is so strong, it still holds up today. The composition has been tested, but never reproduced. Some researchers also have been fascinated at the energy levels found inside the pyramid chambers, and they believe the pyramid shape becomes a type of energy capacitor.

The Great Pyramid has three burial chambers, including chambers for both a king and a queen. The king's chamber was placed in the center of the pyramid and was accessed by walking through a long, granite-lined grand gallery.

Why would a pharaoh spend so much time and so many resources to build a death monument for himself? Perhaps it is because the pharaohs were not thought to be just kings and leaders; the Egyptians also considered each pharaoh a god.

Researchers note that when the Great Pyramid was originally built, the outside was covered with 144,000 polished casing stones. This number is biblically interesting, as Revelation 14:1-3 tells us that 144,000 Jewish men will appear one day on the heavenly Mount Zion.

When the sun hit these highly reflective stones, the pyramid shone like a jewel. It is even suggested that the light from the stones was so bright and powerful, it would have been visible from the moon. Ancient Egyptians called the pyramid "Ikhet," meaning glorious light. An earthquake in the year 1303 loosened and dislodged the stones, at which time many were stolen and used to build temples and mosques.

The Great Pyramid is aligned true north, with accuracy of better than one-fifteenth of one degree. The descending chamber in the pyramid aligned to the North Star when the pyramid was created. The *northern* part of heaven is important biblically, as heaven is located in another galaxy in the northern region of the cosmos (Isa. 14:13; Ps. 48:2; Ezek. 1:4).

From the creation of Adam to the present age is close to six thousand years. Looking at the timeline of both the flood of Noah and the building of the Great Pyramid, it appears that the pyramid was constructed before the flood. It might have been built about the time that Noah was building the ark. This period parallels the time when angels were reproducing with the daughters of men and birthing offspring called "men of renown," or giants (Gen 6:1-4).

Could these giant men have helped moved these massive stones? Could the shape and the cosmic alignments of the pyramid have been revealed by a fallen angel, who had knowledge of cosmic bodies and creation mysteries? Angels would have had astonishing heavenly insight into the cosmic mysteries, long before modern telescopes and NASA space travel.

Another interesting aspect is the controversial meaning of the word *pyramid*. It comes from the Greek words *pyramis* and *pyramidos*. Some suggest the meaning may refer to the shape of the pyramid. However, Egyptologist Mark Lehner researched the ancient meaning of the word for pyramid. He states that it translates as "the place of ascension," referring to the chamber in the pyramid from where the soul of the dead pharaoh was believed to ascend to the afterlife. Others say the word means "fire in the middle," referring to the king's chamber in the center of the pyramid.

It would have taken knowledge or revelation for the Egyptians or someone among them to discover the significance of the pyramid shape and align it so precisely in the building process. However, if we consider that there were angels in human embodiment who would have witnessed the construction of the New Jerusalem, and some of these angels once lived on earth among humans, I think it is possible and even probable that the pyramid formation was designed by them to be a *miniature replica of the heavenly New Jerusalem*.

The pharaohs were considered gods on earth, and the Egyptians believed in an afterlife in which the soul migrates to another realm. The pharaohs' bodies and their wealth were encased in the inner chambers of the pyramid, with the belief that everything buried with them would transfer to the next life.

In Moses' commentary on Noah's day, the deadly flood occurred because of the corruption, violence, and wicked imaginations of men who were inspired by the ungodly offspring that had corrupted the earth (Gen. 6:5, 11, 13). In Noah's day, men had become "gods," and "gods" (angels) had become men.

I suggest that the fallen angels that roamed the earth prior to the flood would have had knowledge of the Holy City in heaven, and they may have attempted to replicate it through the numerous pyramids built, not only in Egypt, but throughout the world.

Interestingly, for some unknown reason, the capstone is missing from the top of the Great Pyramid. It was believed that a capstone was prepared for the top, but it was rejected by the builders. This in interesting, considering a prophecy concerning Christ:

"The stone which the builders rejected
Has become the chief cornerstone."

– Psalms 118:22

"Jesus said to them, 'Have you never read in the Scriptures:

The stone which the builders rejected
Has become the chief cornerstone.
This was the Lord's doing,
And it is marvelous in our eyes'?"

– Matthew 21:42

Before Satan fell, he was a bearer of light—called a morning star. He would have been in heaven when the Holy City of New Jerusalem was being constructed. Just as the Great Pyramid is missing its capstone, I believe it is possible that Satan fell from heaven before the upper section of the New Jerusalem was completed.

The original light bearer in heaven, named Lucifer or Satan, never completed the building project on the New Jerusalem. He was expelled before the upper stones were set in place in the walls. The rejected capstone of the Great Pyramid is missing, while Christ, the rejected stone, has become the Chief Cornerstone of the kingdom! The fallen morning star is no longer a bearer of light; he has been replaced by Christ, the morning star who will one day light the entire city of New Jerusalem from within.

THE LIGHT OF THE CITY

John was told that the New Jerusalem will not require the sun or moon to provide light, as the glory of God and the Christ are the radiance and illumination of the city (Rev. 21:23).

If the city is a cube with twelve separate foundations and floors, each being 1,500 miles square, from a natural perspective, it's hard to imagine how Christ can illuminate twelve separate floors.

Now picture the New Jerusalem as a four-sided pyramid, 1,500 miles square at the base, rising at an angle until it reaches a point, 1,500 miles into the atmosphere, with a capstone at the peak. As a pyramid formation, the light can descend from the top capstone and radiate throughout the city to the foundational level.

The Bible continually uses the word "crystal" to describe the beauty of the throne room, the New Jerusalem, and the river of life (Rev. 4:6; 21:11; 22:1). Most people have seen high quality crystal in the form of expensive glassware and have observed its clarity and brilliance. We can only imagine the brilliance of the city of New Jerusalem.

HOW BIG IS 1,500-MILES-SQUARE?

Taking a map of the United States, if the 1,500-mile-square foundation of the New Jerusalem were placed in America, it would stretch from the east coast of Virginia to the middle of the state of Colorado, and from the bottom tip of Florida to the top of Maine.

When the city descends to earth after the purification of the earth by fire, assuming the land mass remains the same, which continent would the city rest on for all eternity? Since it is the New Jerusalem, it will replace the earthly Jerusalem. But the current city of Jerusalem, and even the square miles within the nation of Israel, is too small for such a massive city.

However, when God made His covenant with Abraham and promised the patriarch a land grant, giving him everywhere the soles of his feet would touch, God then gave the precise location of the land Abraham's descendants would inherit:

"On the same day the Lord made a covenant with Abram, saying: "To your descendants I have given this land, from the river of Egypt to the great river, the River Euphrates..."

– GENESIS 15:18-19

In the time of David and Solomon, the kingdom of Israel expanded south to the river Shihor (called the River of Egypt). This river bordered modern day Egypt and Israel, then ran northward into Lebanon and Syria, and extended to Damascus (2 Sam. 8:3; 2 Chron. 9:26). The promise of the future land grant also extends into the tribal region of parts of Arabia.

To cross from this river to the southern end of the Euphrates today would require passing through a third of Egypt, the Red Sea, Saudi Arabia, and half of Iraq. The New Jerusalem could possibly descend in the land called the Middle East, within the same boundaries promised to Abraham over 4,000 years ago.

When the time arrives for the New Jerusalem to come down out of heaven, the landscape will be completely altered from its present condition, just as Noah's flood changed the surface of the planet. The intense heat from the fiery renovation of the earth will evaporate the oceans, as on the new earth, there is no more sea (Rev. 21:1). The main water source will be the crystal-clear River of Life flowing within the Holy City (Rev. 22:1-2).

The light emanating from within the New Jerusalem will be the reflection of God's glory from within. Using the four-sided pyramid imagery, if we place the throne of God and Christ in the position of the capstone, with the rays of glorious light shooting forth into all four corners of the base foundation, we can see how the entire structure would be lit with the light of the Lamb of God. Now picture a crystal-clear river that might begin 1,500 miles high and cascade downward to the foundation of the city.

We certainly cannot imagine the stunning beauty and possibilities of things to come. One day the New Jerusalem will be the eternal home of the saints of all ages, the holy angels, and Christ Himself.

Growing up in church, we heard songs and sermons based on Christ's words in John 14:1-3 (NKJV):

> *"Let not your heart be troubled; you believe in God, believe also in Me. In My Father's house are many mansions; if it were not so, I would have told you. I go to prepare a place for you. And if I go and prepare a place for you, I will come again and receive you to Myself; that where I am, there you may be also."*

Since the mansions already existed, and since Scripture does not say that Jesus is going to prepare mansions for us, what *place* was Christ preparing for us?

From the fall of Adam until the time of the crucifixion and resurrection of Christ, the spirits of righteous men were taken into a chamber in the underworld called Abraham's bosom (Luke 16:19-23). When Christ was raised from the dead, He led those captives into freedom and brought their souls into paradise in the third heaven. His death and resurrection prepared us a *place* in heaven. Living men required an earthly high priest to make intercession for their sins. Christ opened direct access to God, and one day He will take us from this earth to His heavenly dwelling.

CHAPTER 13

THE ARRIVAL OF THE NEW JERUSALEM

Toward the conclusion of the thousand-year reign of Christ, a sudden and prearranged event will occur. John records that Satan will be loosed from the abyss and will attempt to raise up an earthly army of men to deceive the nations of the earth (Rev. 20:3, 7-9). This is not his great escape, but God will permit Satan for go forth and find some who, oddly enough, will be deceived into thinking they can overthrow Christ and seize His throne. It is a repeat of Satan's attempted coup in ages past, when he believed that he could exalt his throne above the stars of God and become like God (Isa. 14:13-15).

John said that Satan and the armies would surround the "camp of the saints" (Rev. 20:7-9). The Greek word *camp* here is more than a place where people live together. It carries the idea of army barracks, or an encampment that is prepared for war. This indicates that the saints of God (those who returned with Christ as the armies of heaven in Revelation 19), are preparing for Satan to lead his human and demonic hordes in a final assault. As always, Satan overplays his hand, and this time his army is scorched to ashes on the mountains surrounding Jerusalem.

Isaiah warned that Satan would be "brought down to hell, to the sides of the pit" (Isa. 14:15). This will be fulfilled when Satan is cast into the bottomless pit for a thousand years. However, God allows Satan one last stand before his final demise and eternal confinement in the lake of fire.

Why does God allow Satan to be loosed on the earth again for one final attack? The reason might be summed up in the following.

Satan and his dark agents are the source of all evil, temptation, sickness, fear, oppression, and every negative spiritual, physical, and emotional attack. During Christ's thousand-year reign, Satan and his principalities, powers, rulers of darkness, and wicked spirits in high places (Eph. 6:12) have been locked up and kept from assaulting or tempting the earth's population. It would be unjust for humans who repopulated the earth *not to be tested or tempted* in some manner, as we were in our time on earth.

Humans who repopulated the earth can still sin in the millennium, as all humanity is born with a sin nature. Satan will be loosed to test and attempt to deceive the hearts of these men and women, the population of which will likely be in the billions by that time. It is baffling how that, after seeing Christ and worshipping in Jerusalem, a large group of people—the number which is as the sand of the sea—will surround the camp of the saints and the beloved city Jerusalem (Rev. 20:7-9). God will wipe out this massive coalition of rebels with fire out of heaven, devouring them in one swift judgment.

WILL WE BE TEMPTED TO FALL?

Satan was an anointed cherub who was perfect in his ways from the day he was created, until iniquity was found in him (Ezekiel 28:14-15). He was lifted up (haughty) because of his beauty (Ezek. 28:17).

In ages past, heaven's spirit-bodied angels were perfect, yet a third fell into rebellion and were separated from God (Rev. 12:4). The saints of God will have resurrected bodies, called "the spirits of just (righteous) men made perfect" (Heb. 12:23). However, when Satan is loosed, is it possible for some of the resurrected saints to be deceived and fall with Satan, since so many humans, "whose number is as the sands of the sea," will follow Satan after he rises from his abyss? The answer is no.

A true follower of Christ experiences a three-part process. First is *justification through repentance*. When you repent and turn from your sins (John 3:3), you become justified in the eyes of God, which means that you are vindicated and brought in right relationship with Him (1 Cor. 6:11). The Greek word "justify" means to be (legally) acquitted and set free.

The second part of the process is *sanctification*, a word used in the New Testament that means "made holy, set apart for active dedication and service to God" (Rom. 15:16). Justification is through faith, while sanctification occurs by the Word and through the Holy Spirit.

The third and final phase is *glorification*, in which each follower of Christ receives a new resurrected body at Christ's return. When Christ resurrected, His same body was raised from the dead, but it was in a new and better form. He could walk through closed doors (John 20:19-20). He had the unique ability to appear, then suddenly disappear (see Luke 24:31). He could transport His glorified body from one location to another by thought, indicating to us that a glorified body operates beyond the limitations of time and space.

Presently in our bodies of flesh, we have the potential to sin. Our flesh is weak, and the Holy Spirit must work in cooperation with our willpower to keep us from yielding to temptation. However, once we receive a glorified, incorruptible, and resurrected body, we can operate in the same manner that Christ did in His body (1 Cor. 15:50-54). Therefore, in the millennium and beyond, the *presence* of sin is removed and the *power* to sin is made void. In His earthly body, Christ was tempted in all points as we are, yet He did not sin (Heb. 4:15). Since Christ's resurrection, Satan the tempter has and never will have any power, authority, or influence to tempt or test Christ. This is one of the many benefits of the resurrection.

THE JUDGMENT

After this comes the Great White Throne Judgment. There is no indication of the length of this judgment, but billions of people will be judged. This is where the wicked, the godless, and the sinners, including all who died during the thousand-year reign of Christ, will be judged, each according to their works. The Book of Life will be opened to see if their names are inscribed in the book.

When this judgment concludes, the sinners and non-believers—those whose names are not found in the Book of Life—will be separated and sent to the lake of fire. Scripture indicates that this lake of fire will be within the earth. The following verses in Isaiah confirm this:

> "For as the new heavens and the new earth, which I will make, shall remain before me, saith the LORD, So shall your seed and your name remain. And it shall come to pass, that from one new moon to another, and from one Sabbath to another, shall all flesh come to worship before me, saith the LORD. And they shall go forth, and look upon the carcasses of the men that have transgressed against me: for their worm shall not die, neither shall their fire be quenched; and they shall be an abhorring unto all flesh."
>
> – Isaiah 66:22-24 (JKV)

When the New Jerusalem comes to the new earth, there will be an opening in the earth that a person can look into and view the lake of fire. No specific reason is given for this. We know this is hell or the lake of fire because of the phrase, "their worm shall not die, neither shall their fire be quenched," which is the exact warning of hell that Jesus spoke of that was recorded in Mark 9:44-48.

Following the Great White Throne Judgment, God will create new heavens and a new earth. The biblical prophet Isaiah first revealed the coming new heavens and earth:

> "For behold, I create new heavens and a new earth; and the former shall not be remembered or come to mind."
>
> — ISAIAH 65:17 (NKJV)

> "For as the new heavens and the new earth which I will make shall remain before Me," says the LORD, "So shall your descendants and your name remain. And it shall come to pass that from one New Moon to another, and from one Sabbath to another, all flesh shall come to worship before Me," says the LORD."
>
> — ISAIAH 66:22-23 (NKJV)

Christ Himself alluded to this when He wrote, "Heaven and earth shall pass away..." (Matt. 24:35). In the same manner that our bodies will change from mortal to immortal, the old heavens and earth will be transformed from their current form to a new form.

The new heavens and earth appear after death and hell are cast into the lake of fire, and after Satan, the fallen angels, and all demonic spirits are forever cast into this fiery pit, where they will be tormented day and night, forever and ever.

In the chronology John gives us, Satan is cast into the lake of fire with the antichrist and false prophet after he attempts to make war against Christ and the saints in Jerusalem. Then the accuser of the saints before God (Rev. 12:10) will be removed for good, never to be seen or heard from again (Rev. 20:10). The fallen angels are brought out from tartarus, the Greek word for hell in 2 Peter 2:4, where they are now reserved for the final judgment.

God is called "the Judge of all" (Heb. 12:23). At the present time, no angel has ever stood before God to be judged, but Paul noted that the saints of God will judge the angels (1 Cor. 6:3).

Why must the unrighteous dead be judged? God is a just and righteous judge. He will never confine a man, woman, or fallen angel to an eternal prison without first providing them a trial and presenting the evidence against them. At the Judgment Seat of Christ and the Great White Throne Judgment, the books are opened (Rev. 20:12). In any court, the prosecutor presents solid evidence when he argues his case. The evidence can find the person guilty before the judge, which requires a penalty. Some penalties are so severe, they require life in prison or even the death sentence.

Jesus said, "By your words you will be justified, and by your words you will be condemned" (Matt. 12:37). Philippians 3:20 tells us, "For our conversation is in heaven...." Your life's conduct and words will tell the story, as God has your records stored at the tabernacle of the testimony in heaven (Rev. 15:5). When God, as the Judge, reveals the life evidence, none will be able to say, "The charges of God were not true," as the books of heaven do not lie.

THE RENOVATION OF THE UNIVERSE

Once these souls are confined to the lake of fire (Rev. 21:8), God completes the final part of His eternal plan—the creation of new heavens and a new earth, as old things will pass away (Matt. 24:35; Rev. 21:1). The Apostle Peter revealed what will occur when God enacts a complete renovation of the cosmic universe:

> *"But the day of the Lord will come as a thief in the night, in which the heavens will pass away with a great noise, and the elements will melt with fervent heat; both the earth and the works that are in it will be burned up. Therefore, since all these*

things will be dissolved, what manner of persons ought you to be in holy conduct and godliness, looking for and hastening the coming of the day of God, because of which the heavens will be dissolved, being on fire, and the elements will melt with fervent heat? Nevertheless, we, according to His promise, look for new heavens and a new earth in which righteousness dwells."

– 2 Peter 3:10-13 (NKJV)

The Jewish historian Josephus wrote that God warned Adam that the earth would be destroyed in two judgments—once by water and the second time by fire. The Day of the Lord will initiate a judgment by fire, such as in the case of the destruction of mystery Babylon (Rev. 17-18). The sun also will scorch men with great heat (Rev. 16:8-9). Then the time will come when, with a great noise, the heavens "will be dissolved, being on fire, and the elements will melt with fervent heat." The earth and works that are in it will be burned up.

Through God all things consist (hold together – Col. 1:17), so it stands to reason that God also has the ability to make things come apart. Will He use His laws of physics to undo the structure of heaven and earth? Will it happen through some type of nuclear fission that causes flames of fire from one end to the next? We can only speculate about the method God will use to accomplish this. Whatever form He uses, God will send holy fire that cleanses everything so that it can be reformed into a Garden of Eden type of earth.

THE NEW JERUSALEM

The *end* will be a *new beginning*. Not the beginning of a new age or a new dispensation, but the beginning of eternity. The word *eternity* is found only one time in Scripture. In Isaiah 57:15, the prophet wrote of "the High and Lofty One Who inhabits eternity." The word refers to the future, when time will no longer exist.

The word *eternal* is found in forty-five New Testament references. In Greek the word can mean "everlasting, evermore, since the world began." Sometimes the word is translated "ages," such as in Ephesians 2:7, where Paul spoke of "the ages to come." In the sense of eternal life, "eternal" means perpetual, everlasting, and without end. Paul used this term when he spoke of Christ receiving glory "throughout all ages, world without end" (Eph. 3:21 KJV).

God declared to John that He would make all things new. John wrote:

> *"Now I saw a new heaven and a new earth, for the first heaven and the first earth had passed away. Also there was no more sea. Then I, John, saw the holy city, New Jerusalem, coming down out of heaven from God, prepared as a bride adorned for her husband. And I heard a loud voice from heaven saying, "Behold, the tabernacle of God is with men, and He will dwell with them, and they shall be His people. God Himself will be with them and be their God. And God will wipe away every tear from their eyes; there shall be no more death, nor sorrow, nor crying. There shall be no more pain, for the former things have passed away."*
>
> — Revelation 21:1-4 (NKJV)

Notice that all tears will be wiped away, and there will be no more sorrow or crying. There will never be another funeral because there will be no more death. The former things are passed away. The former things passing away means that they depart. They pass completely out of your mind and go away. Former memories are washed away, much like the hard drive of a computer that can be erased of information. As difficult as this seems now, there will be no recollection of any family members who died lost and are separated from you. Painful memories will be erased.

Within the New Jerusalem will be the tree of life and the pure water of life (Rev. 22:1-2). In the Garden of Eden, the fruit from the tree of life extended the health and life of Adam and Eve. Whatever is in this fruit has a supernatural, life-giving element. The water of life will flow out of the throne of God. This water will also have life-giving properties that bring refreshing restoration to all who drink. When the Holy Spirit fills a human spirit, Jesus said that "out of your belly will flow rivers of living water" (John 7:38). Nobody has a literal stream of clear water flowing from their belly, but the point is that the energy and life of God flows from within, just as water flows.

Some suggest that the sun, moon, and stars will no longer exist after this renovation. They base this on Revelation 21:23 which reads, "The city (new Jerusalem) had no need of the sun, neither of the moon, to shine in it: for the glory of God did lighten it, and the Lamb is the light thereof." Here John is speaking of the light shining inside the city, and not the outside of the city or the rest of the world. Outside the city, the sun, moon, and stars continue to exist. The gates to the city will be open continually, as there is no darkness or night inside the massive city.

One of the most unusual verses related to the New Jerusalem reads: "And the nations of them which are saved shall walk in the light of it: and the kings of the earth do bring their glory and honor into it" (Rev. 21:24 KJV). This indicates that nations and kings will walk within the city. These are the righteous, and it appears that the majority of activity happens inside the city. We are not just spirits floating within the massive structure; we are living people who will work and worship.

Activity outside of the city is somewhat of a mystery. However, we know that there will be no more kingdom of Satan and no more rebellious people living on the planet. It will be a new earth, where complete righteousness will dwell.

From the moment you were conceived, you were created with an eternal spirit sent from God that longs to find its way back to God. Once you are born, as you live your life on this earth, you alone will determine where your spirit spends eternity. If you choose to follow Christ, life in the New Jerusalem on the new earth will be your future for eternity. If you reject Christ, your eternal outcome will be completely different. The next chapter will illustrate.

CHAPTER 14

WHAT IF GOD SAID YES TO THE DEAD?

In a book dealing with life beyond death and the future world for those in covenant with God and Christ, something must be said about the netherworld—that is, the underworld, the abyss, or the common word, hell. Some consider the idea of hell a religious myth, a spiritual metaphor, or an allegory. Both Old and New Testaments mention the place, with the first mention in Deuteronomy 32:22: "For a fire is kindled in mine anger, and shall burn unto the lowest hell, and shall consume the earth with her increase, and set on fire the foundations of the mountains."

Hell is beneath (Isa. 14:9), is always down (Isa. 14:15; Ezek. 31:16), and is under the crust of the earth, called "the foundation of the mountains." Hell was not intended to be created for man. Christ revealed that hell was originally prepared for the devil and his angels (Matt. 25:41). In 2 Peter 2:4, Peter revealed that fallen angels are now bound in chains of darkness in hell. In this reference the Greek word for hell is *tartarus*, which among the Greeks was a deep pit or abyss used as a prison to confine the wicked. In this case, it confines the fallen angels.

Jesus presented to His listeners a true story of a rich man who died and found himself in hell. Some suggest this is a parable. However, this story found in Luke 16:19-31 does not have the same illustrative style required for a New Testament parable. This was an actual event, where a rich man would not feed a beggar at his gate. Both died, and one went to the underground location called Abraham's bosom, while the rich man went to hell. A great chasm separated them. Somehow the rich man was able to speak with Abraham.

WARN MY FIVE BROTHERS

This unnamed rich man whose eternal spirit was confined in the netherworld made a strange request. The story was told by Christ to emphasize that your earthly wealth will be worthless in the afterlife, and the way you treated those who are poor and suffering will be remembered beyond the grave. Christ would have been fully aware of this encounter, as He preexisted in ages past (John 8:58).

In Luke 16:19-31, the owner of a wealthy estate had an unwelcomed visitor at his gate. The man was dressed in rags and was weak, poor, and hungry. His name was Lazarus. The only compassion he received was from dogs when they spotted him and came to lick the sores covering his body. The rich man was repulsed by this sickly fellow and would not even hand him a plate of crumbs from his table. In the narrative, both men died, seemingly around the same time. However, their destinations in the afterlife were as opposite as day and night.

Even though the sore-covered body of Lazarus remained on the ground after he died and was moved to some unknown location, angels carried the soul and spirit of the poor beggar to a compartment located underneath the earth called Abraham's bosom (Luke 16:22). The Greek word *bosom* is *kolpos*, which alluded to the breast, or more specifically, the excessive fabric of a tunic that hangs folded over the front. It metaphorically refers to a place of comfort, just as a mother would cuddle an infant close to her breast. This underground location was named after Abraham, as he was the father of the Hebrews.

The rich man didn't fare so well in the afterlife. His soul and spirit left his body and encountered a different eternal abode. Jesus said, "In hell he lift up his eyes, being in torments" (Luke 16:23 KJV). Notice that he had to look up from his place in the lower chamber to see the ledge of the place called Abraham's bosom.

The second observation is the plural word *torments,* meaning different types of torment. The word *torments* is the Greek word *basanos,* and it carries several different meanings. In this case, it refers to severe pain and torture. That would include a painful disease racking someone's body, but in the context of this story, the rich man's soul is sensing torment in hell. His torments included a flame that was burning, a parched tongue that needed water, and the thought that he had family members still living who *had no knowledge of where he was spending eternity.* That brings us to the point.

WARN MY FAMILY

There was a great chasm between this rich man and Abraham and Lazarus. Jesus revealed that the rich man made a request to Abraham, as recorded in Luke 16:27-28. The rich man asked Abraham to send Lazarus to his father's house and warn his five brothers not to come to this place of torment.

Abraham was a guardian of Abraham's bosom, but he had no power to raise anyone, including Lazarus, from the dead, or to send someone back to earth to warn people about hell. That power belonged only to God. Abraham reminded the rich man that, on earth, his brothers had access to Moses (meaning the Torah—the first five books of Scripture written by Moses), along with the writings of the prophets. If his five siblings did not believe the inspired word of God, they would not believe someone who came back from the dead.

This fact was evident when Christ raised another man named

Lazarus from the dead, four days after Lazarus had died. Many Jews then believed that Christ was the Messiah, but others became so angry they wanted to kill Lazarus to destroy the evidence of Christ's miracle-working power. This proves that miracles do not convince everyone (John 11:1-53 and 12:9-11).

However, what if? What if Lazarus had been carried back to earth in his spirit body to appear in front of the five brothers? Follow me along a journey of the beggar and the five brothers, if God had said yes to the dead man's request. Using the idea that Abraham could have sent Lazarus back, I present an imaginative story: What if God had said yes to the dead?

THE VISIT FROM A MAN WHO DIED

Imagine that the spirit of Lazarus suddenly ascends from its subterranean chamber. His spirit passes through the gate at the rich man's home and walks through the carved wooden front door and into the elaborate mansion to warn the rich man's five brothers. What might be their reaction?

As the ghostly figure of Lazarus, whose spirit body might be wrapped in a burial shroud with his head covered and his face barely visible, appears in a large scroll library owned by the oldest brother. The brother is standing over a long, intricately carved wooden table as he carefully reviews unrolled scrolls. Suddenly a deep voice booms from Lazarus, filling the room like approaching thunder. "Your brother is now eternally confined to hell. I am back from the dead to warn you to repent and avoid this terrible place."

Startled, the brother stares for a moment before replying to this stranger, "I am a Pharisee. I am dedicated to the Torah and the Law; therefore, I am righteous. I fast twice a week and pay tithes. I will never go to hell. Whatever you are, whoever you are, your shallow threat of eternal doom is not for me. Take your message and hop over to someone who needs it!"

This brother, as with most devout Pharisees in his day, was stuck in the mud of self-righteousness with a belligerence toward supernatural manifestations that he could not explain.

His sin was pride.

In a room at the opposite end of the house, sitting in a hand-carved cedar chair surrounded by burning oil lamps is the second brother reading from a scroll. He senses a strange presence, looks up, and is stunned to see the image of a man in the room who never entered through the door. He shouts, "Who are you? And how did you get in here?"

Lazarus replies, "I am the beggar who died at your door—hungry, thirsty, and sick. I was sent at the request of your brother, who is now confined to hell, to warn you to repent and not end up where he is!"

The man jumps from his seat, shakes his fist, and replies, "I am a Sadducee. I do not believe in life after death, nor angels, nor demons. Once you are dead, you are dead. Humans do not have an eternal spirit. You are either some apparition playing games with my mind, or you snuck into my house to play a childish trick. I am not fooled. My brother's grave is in the back of this estate, so go tell his corpse your stories."

His sin was unbelief.

In another part of this mansion, the third brother had settled at a large, wooden desk. Clay oil lamps dimly lit several papers, where he was bent over as though closely examining every word. This brother prided himself on his intellect and ability to analyze and resolve difficult situations. He was often overheard bragging, "I am paid bags of silver and gold to solve problems."

In an instant, Lazarus appeared and stood in the middle of the room. For a few moments he stared at the man behind the desk, who was so engrossed in his work that he didn't know anybody was in the room.

Lazarus interrupted the man's thoughts. "I am the old beggar who died at your gate on this property. My spirit has returned from the realm of departed souls to bring a warning from your brother. He is being tormented in hell and is hoping you will turn your heart toward God and repent while you have time.

Slowly staring at Lazarus, the man said nothing. Then he stood up and replied, "Whatever you are, you cannot be real, because hell does not exist. People can believe whatever they want, because God is love and everyone will be fine when they die. My brother worked hard all his life. That is why we are wealthy. He is not in your imaginary hell, so whoever you are, go back to where you came from." Ignoring the supernatural manifestation, the man went back to work, as though nothing happened.

This man's sin was deception.

It was time to approach the fourth brother, a famous merchant who oversaw trade in various towns and cities. Through shrewd business tactics, he had acquired a considerable portfolio, including ownership of some large trade boats used to deliver goods throughout Asia Minor. He had opened shops in several cities, including a bakery that was exceeding expectations. He was pacing the floor, thinking about several Phoenician contracts he was soon to sign.

Suddenly he looked up and caught a glimpse of a ghostly figure walking toward him through a closed door. He stopped in his tracks when he saw the image of a man standing about ten feet away. The figure spoke. "I am Lazarus. You know me. In my previous life I asked the owner of this house for crumbs from his table. He laughed at me. When he died, he was carried into hell. He is there now. Father Abraham sent me back because your brother asked me to come and warn you to repent of your sins and follow the covenant of the Lord;

or else, one day you will be with your brother in this place of torment."

The brother immediately answered, "I don't have time for scare tactics or tall tales. I am a busy man. I work hard, I make money, I travel all of Asia, and I party hard. I have the best and I will enjoy the best. I have plenty of time to repent."

Lazarus replied, "You may be planning to build barns for your wealth and expand your estate. But one day, your soul will be required of you."

The fourth brother ordered Lazarus to go away. "And if you see my brother," he said, "tell him that one day we can party in hell."

The fourth brother's sin was greed, selfishness, and the love of money, which is the root of all evil (1 Tim. 6:10).

One brother remained—the youngest. He had used his wealth to become addicted to strange drugs and drunk with wine. In his drunkenness and incoherence, he often could not work, and his brothers had little to do with him. As Lazarus approached, he observed that the young man was lying on a silk covered couch trimmed with ivory.

As Lazarus stood arms-length away and towering over the youngest brother, the young man rubbed his eyes, shook his head, and rubbed his eyes again. He yelled, "Man, I am tripping out?"

That is when Lazarus spoke. "Do you remember me? You walked past me at your front gate and spat on me. I was sick, starving, and begging for a few breadcrumbs from your table. Your family gave me nothing. When your brother died, his soul went to hell. It is a terrible place, and he is being tormented. He asked that Father Abraham allow me to come and warn his brothers to turn to God, repent, and seek after righteousness. If you do, you will avoid hell. If not, one day you will suffer his same fate."

The young man sat up on the couch. "Man, a ghost is talking to me. Dude, you must be a fog in my brain. I will not go to hell, that is, if hell exists, because I am as good as any other Jew, including my hypocritical and judgmental brothers. Religion divides people. Get out of my face!" He continued to rub his eyes and shake his head, hoping to erase this apparent drug-induced mirage.

The assignment was complete. Lazarus returned to his subterranean home with a sad report. No converts. No repentance. Only belligerence. Without change, all five brothers were headed, at the time of their deaths, to this same eternal prison where they once again would join their older sibling.

In my illustration, no brother repented. In the actual story that Jesus told, we do not know if any brother eventually repented, as Lazarus remained in Abraham's bosom, right where he was. His spirit was not sent to warn the brothers. It is possible that all six men might be confined in hell, where they have been for thousands of years. There is no clock to tell them how long it has been. It is just time without end.

You, too, must choose. There always have been two choices. Before Satan was expelled from heaven, he could have chosen to follow God or lead a rebellion. In the Garden of Eden were two trees: one produced life and one produced death. Adam and Eve had a choice—life or death. The same was true with Israel. God reminded them, "Choose this day whom you will serve" (Josh. 24:15). The entire nation could choose life by obeying the rules of God in heaven, or choose death, through sin and willful disobedience.

Christ came that we could have both abundant life and eternal life. Abundant life is a life choice, but eternal life is a gift. However, you must *choose* Christ. Through His death and resurrection, He has provided a new covenant that offers the gift of eternal life to all who will repent of their sins and receive Him as Savior and Lord. Jesus Christ is more than an eternal fire insurance policy that keeps you out of hell. As Savior, He has purchased your eternal redemption. As Lord, He has blessed you with abundant life.

CHAPTER 15

WILL THE CIRCLE BE UNBROKEN?

It has been one of country music's classic and often recorded songs. Performances at the Grand Ole Opry in Nashville, Tennessee opened and closed with this song. When the Grand Ole Opry played its last show at the Ryman Auditorium before moving to its present location, Johnny and June Cash sang the song to end the final broadcast from the Ryman. In 2010, a terrible flood devastated downtown Nashville, damaging the Opry building. When the building reopened, the first song that was sung was that country and gospel music classic: Will the Circle Be Unbroken?

My Grandad Bava was a minister, as well as a singer, musician, and songwriter. He published and at one time held over a thousand copyrights to songs. He knew many of the early country and gospel singers, some of whom recorded on his two record labels. In his day, everybody in the music industry knew that song.

The song begins with a person looking out the window on a dreary day, observing the funeral hearse carrying their mother away. As a child, I heard it on the radio and elsewhere many times, and I imagined that death had come and someone's loved one was about to be buried. The song talks about a better home awaiting in the sky. To me, the "circle" was the family circle. Momma departed, hoping that when her children and loved ones pass, they will be prepared to meet God and reunite with her in heaven. That is the only way the family circle will not be broken.

I now have great-grandparents, grandparents, and my parents with the Lord, resting and waiting in paradise. I have a sibling I haven't met, and a little girl whose spirit returned to the Lord before she could be born. I don't want anyone who has carried our family name, or who is in our bloodline, or related to me in any manner, to miss spending eternity with the rest of the family. I'm sure every believer feels the same.

Many years ago, I was ministering at Church of the Harvest in Cleveland, Tennessee. I heard Pastor Hank Davis ask the congregation to turn to someone and say, "Heaven would not be the same without you there." The sentence struck my spirit. Thirty years later, I can still hear those words in my head.

There is not one excuse that you can use for not serving Christ. At the heavenly judgment, no excuse will be accepted by God, the Judge. There will be no excuse for how you were raised. No excuse that you were hurt by a preacher or a church. No excuse that there were too many hypocrites in the church. No excuse that you were just too busy or thought you had more time. After the judgment, you will have forever—and that means eternity—to be reminded of why you failed or refused to accept the gift of eternal life and receive Christ's redemptive covenant.

Joshua confronted all the tribes of Israel and demanded that they "choose this day whom you will serve" (Josh. 24:15). We are told that *today* is the day of salvation (2 Cor. 6:2). No person reading this has a guarantee that they will awaken when the sun comes up in the morning.

As for me and my house, we have chosen to serve the Lord. If you are away from Christ or have never trusted Him to forgive you of your sins and become your Lord and Savior, do so today. Don't be the one who breaks the eternal circle. Repent, turn your heart to Christ, pray for mercy and forgiveness, then begin a new journey that will conclude in the ultimate journey that leads to eternal life.